How to Get the Best Employees

Pecuniary and Non-pecuniary Aspects of
Individuals in Labour Market Matching

Table of Contents

1 INTRODUCTION 1

2 HISTORY OF RESEARCH IN THE LABOR MARKET AND NEO-CLASSICAL MATCHING THEORY APPROACHES 2

   2.1 HISTORY OF RESEARCH IN THE LABOR MARKET 2
   2.2 MATCHING THEORY 5
      2.2.1 Becker's basic model of matching 5
      2.2.2 Extension: Assortative matching and Efficient Assignment (matching model with frictions) 10
   2.3 CLASSICAL PRINCIPAL-AGENT-PROBLEM 14
   2.4 WALRAS EQUILIBRIUM AND MATCHING FUNCTION 15

3 PECUNIARY ASPECTS 16

   3.1 LABOR MARKET CONDITIONS 16
      3.1.1 The Real Business Cycle Model 16
      3.1.2 Search Theory 19
      3.1.3 Vacancy Chains as a Contrast of RBC and Search Theory 20
   3.2 QUITTING AND POSITIVE RATE OF RETURN 24
   3.3 SEARCH ON-THE-JOB (OJS) 24
      3.3.1 Acceptance wage 24
      3.3.2 Optimal search strategy 28
   3.4 LAFFER CURVE 30
   3.5 MISMATCHING 32
      3.6 Relative Deprivation Theory 40

4 NON-PECUNIARY ASPECTS 42

   4.1 ORGANIZATIONAL VIEW/EMPLOYER'S VIEW 42
      4.1.1 Recruitment & image of firms as an incentive for workers 42
      4.1.2 Coercion/slavery 50
      4.1.3   Labor Market Matching and Racial Harassment 53
   4.2 WORKERS/EMPLOYEE'S VIEW 55
      4.2.1 Job satisfaction 55
      4.2.2 Quit intentions 58
      4.2.3 Procrastination 64
      4.2.4 Social ties between individuals 66

5   DISCUSSION 70

   5.1   DEPENDENCY OF PECUNIARY AND NON-PECUNIARY ASPECTS OF INDIVIDUALS IN THE LABOR MARKET 71
   5.2   EMPIRICAL EVIDENCE OF PECUNIARY AND NON-PECUNIARY ASPECTS IN THE LABOR MARKET 96
   5.3   IMPORTANCE OF PECUNIARY AND NON-PECUNIARY ASPECTS BY COMPARISON 108

6	RESULT	110
	REFERENCES	114

List of Abbreviations

GSOEP	=	German Socio-Economic panel
ILO	=	International Labor Organization
NHS	=	National Health Service
PIAAC	=	Programme for the International Adult Assessment of Adult Competencies
SME	=	Small and Middle Sized Enterprises

1   Introduction

The process of finding a job is for most employees a difficult one. Logically thinking, many aspects can be a factor of the perception of a job opinion, the remain in one's actually working or maybe even the waiver of any labor. Factors can be the personally situation, different limitations like the limitation of mobility and so on. An often discussed factor of job searching and the decision for an appropriate one is amount of money which one's become for their effort of working. Neo-classical literature debates in several approaches why individuals decide to work in a special company. Mostly, the height of reward in form of money is the key of a decision for one job or another one.

Within the 20th century, real wages increase over time. Furthermore, not only the real wages increase but also the working time for this income decreases. For instance, OECD charts from 1996 and 1998 confirm, that real wages for full-time workers grew between the mid-1980s and the mid-1990s (exception: the USA). For working hours, the opposite is the case. Most OECD countries have a downwards trend from the early 1980s to today. Examples for "falling countries" are Japan, Spain, Germany or France. Some OECD countries stagnate in their working hours like Canada and the UK. There are only two exceptions in this context. On the one hand Sweden and on the other hand on more time the USA (Clark 2005).

So, if the real wages in the most countries increase over the last time and if the working hours in the same time period sink, why are deceases like burnout more topical than ever? Following neo-classical theories, individuals should try to get more money and more leisure time. But it seems that this is not the case to get happier. The factors of pecuniary job decisions are on the one hand a clear and right one. But on the other hand there are more influences on individuals who search, practise or quit a job. So called non-pecuniary factors like job satisfaction, procrastination or coercion are also things who affect a people's choice.

2 History of Research in the Labor Market and Neo-classical Matching Theory Approaches

2.1 History of Research in the Labor Market

The researches why workers choose a certain employer are manifold and questioned by a range of persons. Whereas neo-classical models with pecuniary issues have determined the past, many questions of today are asked in the direction of non-pecuniary aspects.
One early work of the matching of employee and employer is from Becker (Becker 1973). In his paper, he examines with the example of marriage that every individual try to find a partner which is as well as possible. Furthermore, his so called "marriage market" has to be in equilibrium in the end. So, every individual has to find some other individual to match. Becker calls this the "best mate".
In another paper of George Stigler, he dedicates his attention onto the topic of searching. He explains the term "search" in form of buyers

and sellers in a market. To become the best price, buyers respectively sellers have to canvass various sellers (or buyers) (Stigler 1961). In addition, another paper of Phelps observed wage effects of employer and employee. Therefore he assumes an equilibrium in the labor market (Phelps 1968). Within this period, the first papers about non-pecuniary aspects are published. Many of them approach the theme of social ties between actors within the labor market. So, for example studies of Granovetter or Liu and Duff (Liu and Duff 1972, Granovetter 1973).

Another important work about the terms of labor market, again in the pecuniary field, is from Heckman. Within his study, he tries to show the labor market in the light of shadow prices and once again market wages (Heckman 1974). Others concentrate rather on the unemployed than the employed population, for instance the paper of Salop (Salop 1973). He observed the terms of searching of unemployed individuals.

Non-pecuniary aspects are still rare. A paper of Lin, Ensel and Vaughn shine a light on the aspect of social ties (Lin, Ensel et al. 1981). Some papers consecrates now to the reasons for quitting a certain job - as well for males as for females. Examples of those papers are work of Black (Black 1981) or the one of Viscusi (Viscusi 1980). Furthermore, some papers try to include as well pecuniary as non-pecuniary aspects into their analysis. The study of Lee and Wilbur is therefore of importance (Lee and Wilbur 1985). But wage models are part of the scientific improvement of the understandings of the labor market, too. The try of creating efficiency wage models of Akerlof and Yellen is therefore a good example (Akerlof and Yellen 1986).

Within the theories of unemployment, Pissarides implement some interesting but very theoretical models (Pissarides 1990). In addition, authors like McCormick analyses the matching tries of employees (McCormick 1990) Within the matching context, further papers enters the market, for instance one of Hersch (Hersch 1991). She criticises mismatches considering the bridge of an individual between education and job and the following possible over- and undereducation for the work.

With the beginning of the new century, more and more papers take a closer look in the field of non-pecuniary aspects in the labor market context. Examples in the fields of quitting behaviour (Shields and Price 2002, Lévy-Garboua, Montmarquette et al. 2007), job satisfaction (Kristensen and Westergård-Nielsen 2004, Cornelißen 2009) or racial harassment (Bertrand and Mullainathan 2003).

The field of pecuniary theories and especially the theory of matching becomes another paper with the assortative matching version of Shimer and Smith (Shimer and Smith 2000). The results of Becker's theory of marriage in comparison to labor market theories was in this time also extended by Smith (Smith 2006). Matching procedure through terms like friendship or employee referrals is also of great importance (Fernandez, Castilla et al. 2000, Sterling 2014)

All in all, the literature of theories about the labor market becomes bigger over time. Thereby the non-pecuniary aspects of employers as well as employees are observed rather in the newer time. Older literature concentrates rather on neo-classical aspects and pecuniary labor market equilibria. A crucial example therefore is the wage rate theory section.

2.2 Matching Theory

2.2.1 Becker's basic model of matching

With his paper "A Theory of Marriage: Part I", Gary Becker was one of the leaders of the neo-classical tries which want to explain why and how individuals search other individuals as "partners". Becker argues that an individual matches with another one with a view to gain from this partnership. Thus, for instance, two persons marry each other just if both increase their utility.

To show this, Becker explains the matching theory with the above-mentioned example. In his model, he distinguishes between individual M and F. Both decide to marry each other or stay alone. In this context, "marry each other" means to pool the households of M and F into one household. Each household gain commodities partly from goods as well as services of the person and partly from the time the person invests into producing. These commodities are not transferable or marketable between other households but between members of the same household. All commodities like quality of child education, health status or love are concluded into the variable Z. So, Becker set up the equation

$$Z = f(x_1,\ldots,x_m;t_1,\ldots,t_k;E),$$

with x_i as some goods and services, t_i as the time inputs of the household members and E as "environmental" variables.

Thus, the factors goods, times and an environmental variable play a role. Thereby, time T is defined through the equation

$$l_j + t_j = T \quad \text{all } j,$$

where l_j shows the time an individual spends with working in the market sector and T represents the total time of each member. Becker argues that each member of the marriage cooperate within the allocation to help to reach the maximization of the total output Z.

Within a marriage, the factor time T can be separated into T_f for the time of woman and T_m for the time of men. For Becker, the combination of both times, T_f and T_m, leads to 24 hours per day, 168 hours per week, and so on and hence to a maximization of possible time. Furthermore, he suggests that persons who are married work more in the case of a men and less in the case of a woman. Reason for these assumptions is that single men and woman only have to allocate their own time between the market and the non-market sector. Furthermore, single individuals do not have time and goods from their partners. Hence, they have different possibilities than married persons.

Within his paper, Becker develops conditions for marriage, namely

$$m_{mf} \geq Z_{m0}$$
$$f_{mf} \geq Z_{0f}$$

where Z_{m0} and Z_{0f} show the maximum output of a single man respectively woman and m_{mf} and f_{mf} a married man respectively woman. Thus, the condition says that married individuals generate a higher output than single ones. If this is not true, a marriage is useless. Moreover, Becker gives the "necessary condition for marriage", which is

$$m_{mf} + f_{mf} \equiv Z_{mf} \geq Z_{m0} + Z_{0f}.$$

Thus, under these conditions, matching is only useful in materially things. Merging of time and good units and the following allocation is a central reason for marriage. If a possible marriage does not result in a better or equal standing for both partners, a marriage does not come about. Hence, only pecuniary measurable factors count - non-pecuniary aspects are not in focus.

Becker argues in the context of the "marriage equation" that some other factors are quite more important than a better standing in time and goods after a marriage. Over all, the raise of own children is the primary key of a marriage between man and woman. In contrary to a single man respectively woman, individuals in partnerships create the "good" of children. Furthermore, physical and emotional attraction plays a role.

Thus, it seems that there are not only materially reasons for matching in the context of marriage. This can be shown with another example. Becker supposed that individuals who marry each other merge their separate single households in one household. This implicates a reduction in "cost of frequent contact and of resource transfer between each other" (Becker 1973, 819). Hence, with more than one individual, these persons have a gain in working together - an economies of scale effect arises. But a standard marriage consists of one man and one woman. Persons do not look for other individuals to get better economies of scale. Thus, the living of men and women together in a marriage has to go deeper than for the effects of economies of scale.

To understand the advantages of matching in the context of marriage, another assumption is given. For Becker, the time of men and women, t_m and t_f, are not perfect substitutes for other goods or services of market firms or other households. This mean that a unit of t_m can only produced for a certain woman if she has a man and both are married. If the certain woman is a single, she can not get this good t_m at the market for another one or produce it by herself - at least not with the amount of a married woman. Hence, the optimal combination of inputs for t_m (t_f) is only available for married woman (men).

Another important point of a possible match within the Becker model of marriage is the balance between gain and cost. Like for many other examples in life, one has to choose if a marriage has more advantages than disadvantages. In neo-classical contexts, a marriage only comes about if the advantages outweigh the disadvantages. Otherwise, the individuals stay in the single stadium. Within this problem, and considering the main reason of marriage, namely raise children, Becker argues that persons go the rather in the stadium of marriage the higher the importance and "quality" of possible children. Persons, who want only few children or where the chance of "good" children is relatively low, tend to marry later, divorce earlier or do both.

All in all, Becker suggests that marriage is the aim of single individuals. A marriage signals the market equilibrium of two single persons. Reasons therefore are advantages like the good of time t_m and t_f, a better allocation of goods for both because of a merged household or the possibility of raising children. Furthermore, the best form of marriage for Becker is between one man and one woman for one household. More persons have disadvantages like diminishing returns within a household, other forms of relationships (namely two individuals of the same sex) have disadvantages in form of missing t_m respectively t_f.

Becker's model of marriage gives a good example of neo-classical thinking of matching and shows possible approaches for the models of labour market matching with employee and employer as man and woman and, furthermore, a matching as market equilibrium. Although the circumstances of matching in this context are differently from the ones of labour market matching, the basics of matching become more clarity with it.

2.2.2 Extension: Assortative matching and Efficient Assignment (matching model with frictions)

Basing on the above-mentioned paper of Becker, Lones Smith writes down some thoughts about Becker's frictionless model (Smith 2006). In Smith's meaning, matching implies factors like time-consuming search and impatient individuals. With the given further assumptions of Becker of individuals who want to improve their own gain with a matching partner, these matching behaviour creates a "block segregation" where a certain type of individual always match with another certain type. This leads to an amount of blocks of matches between all individuals.

To explain the model with search frictions, a term called "assortative matching" is created. This term means that a match between two individuals arises if a certain individual prefers a higher partner. In this context this means that the "highest" individual is chosen by the second highest, the third highest by the fourth and so on. The certain individual tries to find matches with persons "around" him or her, respectively. Hence, following Smith, for perfectly assortative matching, "the market clears top to bottom" (Smith 2006, S. 1125).

Smith considers another paper by Sattinger who also concentrates on the terms of matching in the labor market. Thereby, he assumes circumstances with heterogeneous jobs and workers and a labor market environment which might lead to multiple equilibria (Sattinger 1995). Within the labor market, employer and employee try to find matches which lead to a maximized output for the certain economy. Therefore, employers create different wage rates. Employees search for jobs with appropriate wage levels to estimate the required abilities for the job. Both parties have to use searching for successful matching because on the one hand, organizations do not know all abilities of the workers and on the other hand, the workers do not know all possible vacancies. But the output of a match depends on the two factors worker and job. Hence, regarding the maximization of output, the economy tries to find perfect matches. Furthermore, the decisions of matching create externalities. Sattinger shows an example why this can happen. If "there is an increase in matches between the least productive workers and jobs of average productivity […] these jobs will no longer be available for matches with workers of average productivity. The loss of these future matches is not directly considered by the worker and employer when they decide to form a match" (Sattinger 1995, S. 283). For Sattinger, externalities occur if a certain match which is formed currently, has compared to forgone future matches of these parties a low output. Hence, employee and employer have to strike up a certain relation to maximize the output of the combination of worker and organization in special and the whole economy output on aggregate. The problem with this is that the nth worker can not wait for the nth job which would be a requirement for the self-selection assignment. Thus, workers formulate a strategy to accept more than one employer, namely a certain range of possible organizations where the employee can work. Employers react in the same way. They accept a range of applicants for a certain vacancy. Orientation for worker and organizations is thereby the rate of wages and the supposed skills or abilities, respectively.

Hence, workers as well as employers use search methods to become their counterpart. Sattinger argues that the term of reservation wage is a crucial point of these search theories. Reservation wage means that for instance a worker search for a certain wage rate and accepts every offer with this rate and above from any employer. The difficulty of this proceeding is that by this way, multiple equilibria might occur. In addition the finally resulting assignment could be not the one which maximizes the output between employee and employer relation. To prevent this situation, another approach is developed. This method incorporates the opportunity costs of worker and employer. Gains and losses are count in who would come from future matches and who are not going to occur with the currently match. So, if decisions of matching are based on the opportunity costs approach, the output of a certain relation can be maximized. However, this method has also a disadvantage. Some opportunity cost levels "differ systematically from the reservation wages and profits" (Sattinger 1995, S. 283). Sattinger gives an example of the reservation wage of the least productive worker. His or her reservation wage exceeds the opportunity costs. Thus, the certain worker would reject matches which might raise the aggregate output of the economy.

Excurse: Contracts between Individuals

Within the matching of the two parties employee and employer in the labor market, contracts seem to play an important role. Considering the paper of Rousseau and McLean Parks, contracts have a widespread conventional wisdom (Rousseau and McLean Parks 1993). Some of these hypotheses are of relevance for the pecuniary and non-pecuniary aspects. For instance, there are several positions about trust. On the one hand, persons assert that contracts create trust and that they are substitutes of trust. But on the other hand some persons suggest that they create mistrust and furthermore that they are a symptom of mistrust in a worker-organization-relationship.

Following Rousseau and McLean Parks, contracts can have two variants. First, the social contract variant is based on cultural factors. "Social contracts are normative, addressing shared, collective beliefs regarding appropriate behaviour in a social unit" (Rousseau and McLean Parks 1993, S. 3). The second one is the promissory contract, which is characterized by "paid for promises". Effort, loyalty, fidelity and others get exchanged for a mostly monetary payoff. This type of contract is the one of normal labor market agreements between employee and employer.

Agreements of both labor market parties through a contract is also part of the agency theory (see 2.3) and transaction cost economies. Considering the case of agency theory, contracts hinder an agent (partly) in shirking. The principal can not see the working effort of the agent. With strike up a contract between principal and agent, the agent promise to do the task of the principal.

2.3 Classical Principal-Agent-Problem

The problem of a principal-agent relationship is broadly discussed in the economic literature. Considering the fact of contracts between individuals, a transfer to the factors of labor market is obvious.

Mainly, the difficulty between the principal and the agent is as follows. A certain principal, in the context of labor market an employer, delegates a task to an agent, so an employee. For doing this task, the principal gives the agent a compensation, normally a certain amount of money. For this wage, the agent accomplishes the task. Main problem of this relation now is that the principal can not see if the agent does his or her work satisfactorily. The certain effort that the agent invest to does the task is unknown by the principal. Most theories of the principal-agent-problem assume that the agent is risk averse.

Holmstrom and Milgrom give a closer view on the functions of a linear principal-agent model (Holmstrom and Milgrom 1991). Thereby, the agent in the relationship takes a one-time choice within a set of vectors $t = (t_1,\ldots,t_n)$ at his or her personal cost $C(t)$. Regarding the reward for working, the effort t of the agent leads to expected gross benefit $B(t)$. In addition, the effort of the agent creates a vector of information signals, namely

$$\chi = \mu(t) + \varepsilon.$$

If the contract with the principal has a compensation in form of the wage w(χ), the expected utility of the agent has the form

$$u(CE) = E\{u[w(\mu(t) + \varepsilon) - C(t)]\}.$$

Thereby, $u(w) = -e^{-rw}$ and CE are the „certainty equivalent" monetary payoff of the agent. The term r is the above-mentioned agent's risk aversion. In contrast, the principal is risk neutral.

2.4 Walras Equilibrium and Matching Function

The Walras equilibrium is one of the most famous economic theories. It is going about that demand and supply of all goods are in one point in equalization. For example, there is person A and person B and good one and good two. Both individuals want some amount of good one and two. Condition here is a price vector. So, both individuals can choose a bundle of goods with their budget. Now they begin to trade until the goods are for both in an acceptable way partitioned and the supply is exhausted. With this allocation, the Walras equilibrium is achieved (Varian and Buchegger 1991, Mas-Colell, Whinston et al. 1995).

Following the theory of Walras equilibrium, this framework is applicable in the context of labour markets, too. Therefore, we have individuals who want to buy and sell their good, namely labour. Individual A is the employer and individual B the employee. So, A wants to buy work and B to sell, respectively.

Based on these theories, a matching function was implemented by Pissarides (Pissarides 1990). Thereby, a matching function is defined by the number of jobs formed at any moment in time. These are the number of workers who are looking for a job plus the number of firms who are looking for workers plus some possible other variables (Pissarides 1990). These jobs can be formed because of the heterogeneity of individuals, here namely workers. Both sides, the possible employers and employees, have to invest. Employers try to find the best educated workers and possible employees want to show themselves and their qualifications.

3   Pecuniary Aspects

3.1   Labor market conditions

3.1.1   The Real Business Cycle Model

The model of business cycles is a macroeconomic one. Within this model, the ups and downs of an economy can be illustrated via peaks and troughs and in between a recession and an expansion phase.

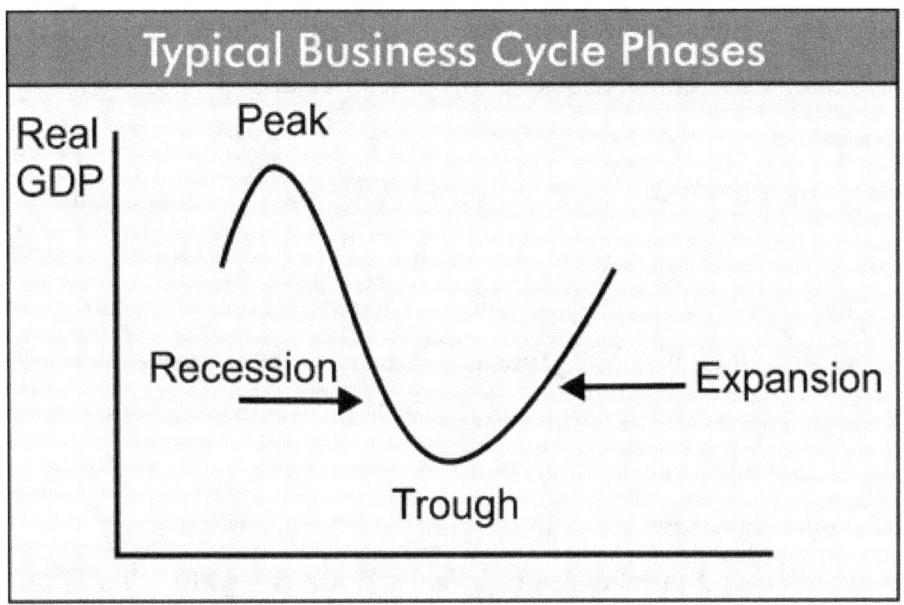

These ups and downs of industries or even economies are mostly explained through technological shocks. Some authors exert this theory in the context of labour markets. In a recession phase until a certain trough, investments of firms sink. Hence, the unemployment is high because the available jobs are low. With starting the expansion phase, firms begin to invest more, so, new jobs are available and the unemployment sinks until the peak of a business cycle. Thus, the rate of unemployment follows the business cycles. Therefore, some authors call the unemployment rate a cyclical one.

One example of these authors are Mortensen and Pissarides and their paper about this theme (Mortensen and Pissarides 1994). They observe the terms job creation and job destruction and their correlations with aggregate and dispersion shocks. Whereas aggregate shocks imply a negative correlation with job creation and destruction, dispersion shocks imply a positive one.

Mortensen and Pissarides assume a model of creating and destroying jobs, which has some very theoretical conditions. There are firms on the one hand and workers on the other. Every created job by the firm has the task to produce one unit of a certain good. Therefore, one worker has to be hire by the firm to interact with the created job and in combination, one unit of good is new in the market. Investments of firms are, once done for a certain job, irreversible. So, every firm in the model has exactly one job. This job can fulfil one of two states, either filled and producing or vacant and searching. If a job is not filled with a worker and also not in the searching process, this job gets destroyed. The profession of the created job is also irreversible (before the creation, the job profession is fully flexible). Furthermore, there is no on-the-job search of workers in this model and workers are either in a modus of unemployment and searching or in a job and producing. To become higher wages, workers have to look for new jobs, because new jobs are always the one with the highest production and therefore the highest wages (see the paragraph below).

If there is a negative shock, the amount of jobs can decline. The moment of destruction is given by the firm but jobs have to be degraded. The positive variant, the creation of jobs, depends on the information for potential employers. New jobs can be created by already existing firms or by new entrants. Mortensen and Pissarides argue, that new job by existing firms are the more productive ones.

Thereby, they lean on empirical evidence from the US labour market, where only 18% of total created jobs account in favour of firms with three years or under in establishment (Davis and Haltiwanger 1991, Mortensen and Pissarides 1994). Furthermore, Mortensen and Pissarides argue that firms which are already for a long time in the market have a better sense for profitable products (within their sectors). Consequently, new created job by this type of firm is a more productive one and thus, given the best technology, jobs which have been created by long existing firms are the most productive ones.

Following from the thesis of idiosyncratic risks of a certain firm and so not from a wide market area, Mortensen and Pissarides assume that the matching process is "between individual job vacancies and unemployed workers, rather than between multiple-job firms and workers" (Mortensen and Pissarides 1994, S. 398).

3.1.2 Search Theory

Within the terms of search theory, in the labor market there are employed individuals and unemployed individuals. Hence, a person can have one of two states. A study of Mortensen explained the main ideas of this theory (Mortensen 1986).

Whereas employed individuals just do their work, unemployed ones just look for a job. The theory of search in the context of labor market conditions assumes that persons, who are not employed, want a job. So, the central question of this theory is not if an individual who is unemployed wants a job but if he or she accepts a certain offer or if he or she rejects it. Hans van Ophem summarized the theory of search, too (Van Ophem 1991). In his paper, he argues that individuals, who are unemployed, weight their costs of searching with the gain they become with a new job. Thereby, the costs can be in form of pecuniary costs like travel-expenses or buying newspapers or in terms of non-pecuniary aspects like mental costs and so on (Van Ophem 1991). The returns of this search are a utility or wage increase for the better job or, in case of job offers without search, through the higher probability of becoming a better job. Based on the assumptions of Mortensen, a searching individual has to compare the utility of his or her current job with a so called reservation utility. This reservation utility is the result of the equalization of all marginal costs and returns of a certain job. If the gain of the reservation utility is for the certain individual higher than the gain of the current job, the person starts to search for another, better job. Thus, the search decision is based on the costs and returns of the current job versus the costs and returns of a desire job.

Considering the fact that the individual try to compares costs some difficulties can occur. Pecuniary and non-pecuniary aspects of a current job can as well be observed as pecuniary aspects of a possible better new job. But non-pecuniary aspects like collegiality, motivation for the new work or the overall satisfaction with the new job can at least considered when the person accept the offer and get the better job.

3.1.3 Vacancy Chains as a Contrast of RBC and Search Theory

An important aspect in the labor market is the employment rate. Many decisions in the working area are dependent from an either high degree of unemployment, hence, many jobless people, lower investments of firms, etc or from the contrary, a high degree of employment. One of these factors, the rate of quits of individuals who are in jobs, was examined by Akerlof, Rose and Yellen (Akerlof, Rose et al. 1988). In their paper, they argue that many people voluntarily quit their jobs when the stage of low unemployment is reached. Therefore, a Keynesian model was implemented. Within this model, jobs are rationed and Akerlof et al. try to explain why quitting behaviour is pro-cyclical.

Therefore, the authors introduce a term called "vacancy chain". Following the theory of Akerlof et al., all individuals want a job. But jobs are rationed. Thus, there are always some people who can not work. At this point, Akerlof et al. determine an important market failure: "a characteristic of equilibrium in models with rigid wages is that some individuals covet jobs held by others who are no better qualified" (Akerlof, Rose et al. 1988, S. 496).

Hence, jobs can only conquered when there are opportunities for the people in jobs. This framework starts the vacancy chain. Following Akerlof et al. in an example, an employee A becomes opportunities and he uses one of them and quits the actually job in favour of another one (so, switch the job). Individual B, who may has another job at this time and covets A's job, has now the opportunity to incurs A's formerly work. This leads to an opportunity for individual C, who coverts B's job, etc. This vacancy effects goes on and on until persons become opportunities who before are unemployed. Akerlof et al. call this "employment to employment job switches" or "E-to-E quits".

The period of a vacancy chain depends on the rate of unemployment in the certain labor market. Vacancy chains in markets with a high unemployment are shorter than ones in markets with a low unemployment. This happens because with high unemployment, the row of individuals who switch jobs until a person comes that does not have a work before, is shorter. If unemployment is low and nearly everyone has a certain work, this cycle continues for a longer time until the unemployed individual comes. This phenomenon also explains why quit rates increase in a labor market with low unemployment rate. With a longer cycle of quits and job switches, more individuals become the chance of opportunities. Hence, more persons can switch the current job to change to the covet one.

Akerlof et al. criticise with their theory of vacancy chains the theories of real business cycles and search theory. For instance, negative shocks in business cycles theory lead to an amount of quits from working individuals. For the business cycle theory, these quits increase the rate of unemployment because individuals quit the labor market. So, aggregate employment and the quit rate are in a negative correlation. Search theory argues that quits and unemployment have a positive correlation. For Akerlof et al. and the vacancy chain theory, these workers have an incentive to voluntarily reallocate them across sectors. Hence, negative shocks do not change the number of workers, hence, the number of jobs and hence, the rate of unemployment (Akerlof, Rose et al. 1988, Mortensen and Pissarides 1994).

A reduction in unemployment raises the welfare. This can be the case because according Akerlof et al. and the vacancy chain theory, individuals search for opportunities. Opportunities can be a higher wage on the one hand or more job satisfaction respectively higher non-pecuniary rewards on the other hand. Individuals prefer in this model different amounts of both goods. Furthermore, the willingness of a certain worker to accept a special job is match-dependent and varies with time. With this background, it is possible that workers choose new opportunities in form of a new vacancy with the possibility of an equal or even lower wage rate. In neo-classical conditions of individuals, aims of work are only money respectively good and leisure time. Thus, under these conditions a negative change in wage amount of a single person would result in a decline of overall welfare. For Akerlof et al., job satisfaction is another important factor of overall welfare. Any "realistic portrait of labor turnover must include a role for nonpecuniary rewards" (Akerlof, Rose et al. 1988, S. 498). Empirical evidence confirms an even higher importance of non-pecuniary rewards in comparison to pecuniary ones. Most quits of jobs are the result of non-pecuniary considerations. As an example, 24 percent of the work force of United States manufacturing quits every year since 1945 (Akerlof, Rose et al. 1988). Such factors like the one of job satisfaction can be considered in section 4.

3.2 Quitting and positive rate of return

Quitting the current job can increase the short-run wages on condition of some aspects. In his paper, Black examines that workers who move from relatively low paid jobs to higher paid jobs if they accomplish these aspects (Black 1980). So, one condition is that these workers have high voluntary labor mobility. This generates a better allocation of labor in the competitive labor market und so a pareto-optimal allocation within the workers and firms.

Another important factor of better jobs is the so called "on-the-job search" (OJS) of individuals (see 3.3). Black argues, following Mattila, that "50%-60% of quitters were able to switch jobs without intervening unemployment" (Mattila 1974, Black 1980, S. 222). This data from 1961 supports the thesis that OJS is a widespread given method to search for new jobs. In contrast, Black also argues that workers without OJS have to accept lower paid job offers than with the help of OJS. Furthermore, workers who will not search on-the-job also do not see existing market wage opportunities as good as workers who search already on-the-job (Black 1980).

3.3 Search on-the-job (OJS)

3.3.1 Acceptance wage

An implication of job searching is the aspect that individuals have to accept the wage rate of new jobs. Therefore, a so called acceptance wage represents a border, which has to be hurdled if one wants to change the job. The acceptance wage illustrates thereby amongst others the costs of search for a new job and the quit activity of an old one (Black 1980).

In his paper, Weiss argues that organizations do not try to pay an applicant a wage which is as low as it can be. The implication of wages for hired workers is rather to pay a wage rate which "minimizes its cost per efficiency unit of labor" (Weiss 1980, S. 527). This is based on the argumentation about labor demand and supply. The approach has two assumptions. First, wages of workers are not proportionate to the productivity of them. Second, the acceptance wages of employees are an increasing function of this productivity. If a firm searches for new workers, there is a certain amount of individuals the firm need. This is the demand of labor of the organization. With determine a wage rate where the firm has to pay a minimum wage, the labor demand of the firm is covered. Following Weiss, the firm can increase the wage rate for a certain position. This results in a higher degree of applicants for the vacancy. In addition, the quality of the pool of applicants increases with this procedure, because higher wages elicit better workers. Hence, the organization can now choose a better skilled person for the job which increases the efficiency of labor in the firm. So, on the one hand, the costs for a further unit of labor is higher but on the other side the gain from this unit is higher, too. All in all, the organization tries to minimize the costs compared to the gains of labor units or workers, respectively.

Another point of view in the paper of Weiss is the one of wage perceptions of rejected job applicants. In the mind of Weiss, the certain applicant who has not become the favourite job should not reduce his or her expected wage rate. Job offers do not increase with a lower wage perception. Firms who try to get a minimized cost per labor unit, set wage offers higher to attract better skilled individuals. With reducing the expected wage rate, a worker declines his chance to get hired because the firm might see in his or her a too low skilled person for the job. Thus, to prevent the worker from long time unemployment, he or she should set the wage rate higher to draw attention to his or her skills.

The theory of minimizing costs per efficiency unit of labor can have some disadvantages. With this practise, an excess of supply of workers for all firms might be developed. Workers who are in job queues could not become offers of firms until their upper bound of acceptance wage is reached. Another disadvantage occurs if the organization has a fall in demand. Quality differences between the workers can not be seen by the firm but they correlate with the expected wage rates of the workers. These expected wage rates is the amount which the workers can receive in other firms of the economy, too. If the certain firm now cut the highest wages, these workers, who also are the ones with the highest qualities or skills, respectively, leave the firm and go to another. Hence, to avoid such behaviour of the high-quality workers, the firm has to fire arbitrarily some employees.

Cost-minimizing wages can also lead to unemployment rates and too high wages. This can be differently for groups within the observed economy. For a given level of aggregate demand, some types of groups can have an excess demand of their abilities. Because workers in these fields are rare, firms tend to pay more than the cost-minimizing wage rate for them. On the other side, if there is an excess in supply, some individuals do not become a job or have to enter job queues for their cost-minimizing wages.

There are several reasons why firms not pay wages proportionate to productivity. The most logical one is that it is too costly to become precise information about the productivity of the worker. The costs of it do not exceed the benefit. Furthermore, firms tend to pay more than necessary, even if they know with certainty the productivity of their workers. Reason therefore is the rate of income taxes. With progressive income taxes, workers might have to pay higher taxes on their income if they receive lower wages.

The question why firms not just pay workers a wage which is proportional to their expected productivity can be easily answered. The reason why this can not happen is given with morale effects. If one considers two workers who perform the same work and one of the worker is more productive than the other one but gets a lower wage rate, morale problems of the worker can occur which impact the effort and so the productivity negatively. Reason for the better paid job of the less productive worker in this case is just that he or she "was believed to be of higher ability" (Weiss 1980, S. 528) at the hiring process than the other worker.

All in all, the theory of acceptance wages has some true statements which might occur in similar cases in the real world context. Especially arguments of quit intention because of wage cuts or false allocation of wages amongst workers and their production seems to be important within the labor market matching.

3.3.2 Optimal search strategy

Following a paper of Morgan and Manning, a strategy of optimal search includes the advantages of different search strategies (Morgan and Manning 1985). Therefore, the rules for optimal search follow the term of expected-utility-maximization. Hence, the searcher chooses as well the number of periods in which samples has to be taken as the size of these samples taken in each period.

Morgan and Manning combine two different theories of search to create the optimal search way. Base for both theories is that a certain searcher observes information periodically from a population until he has found what he wants. A finding stops the search and finished it.

The first strategy is the fixed-sample size. Here, a searcher chooses a total number of observations and then examines each observation in a sequentially procedure. Because this treatment is very inefficient, some authors consider a fixed-sample size strategy where a searcher can draw a certain sample of observations simultaneously (Gal, Landsberger et al. 1981, Benhabib and Bull 1983, Burdett and Judd 1983). An example therefore is given by Morgan and Manning with a Ph.D. graduate who seeks for an academic post. The Ph.D. would rather apply to several universities at once than applies only for one, wait for a positive or negative reply and then maybe continue. Advantage of the fixed-sample size strategy is that an individual can with this gather quicker an amount of information. However, the too much information may result in overinvestment in information.

The second implemented strategy is the sequential search strategy. Within this strategy, a searcher "draws exactly one observation at a time and waits until that observation is received before deciding if he should draw another" (Morgan and Manning 1985, S. 923). Hence, the fully amount of observations is unknown until the needed information is achieved, which results in a stop of searching. Advantage of this method is that no overinvestment can happen. The searcher tries to find his or her information with one observation in each period. If the searcher has what he or she wants, the search stops. The disadvantage is logically the wasted time of searching. With using only one observation in each period, the search process might be a long one for a large sample of possible information.

With the optimal search strategy, the advantages of both methods will be combined. Now, a search has the speed of the fixed-sample size strategy and the flexibility of avoiding unnecessary costs by the sequential search theory.

3.4 Laffer curve

Another pecuniary effect which has to be included in the pecuniary decisions in the labor market and its matching is the influence of taxes on demand and supply of labor. The easiest view of this term is that with a higher rate of labor tax, the demand as well as the supply of labor decline. On the workers view, the supply sinks because workers get less net money from working for the same wage as before. As a result, they might call for a higher wage rate. On organizational view, this leads to less demand, because higher wage claims result in higher costs for a certain firm. Hence, higher tax rates can impede matching in the labor market.

Thus, the solution if this problem could be that there is no tax on labor. But this kind of tax is an important source of income for every state. Without reallocation of this money, no state can finance projects like public goods. A certain tax has to impose on the working population. On the one hand, the amount of tax should not be too low because expenditures have to be covered. But on the other hand, a tax rate which is too high, leads to a decline in demand and supply of labor.

To explain this terms, a method was include, which was called the Laffer curve. The Laffer curve tries to explain the perfect rate of a certain tax, in this context the tax of labor. If the tax rate is zero, the fiscal revenues are zero, too. If the tax rate is 1, the fiscal revenues are also zero (see above). Hence, the rate has to be between these two rates. The particular in tax rating is, that with declining labor demand

and supply, a higher tax rate could reduce the tax income (Varian and Buchegger 1991). Laffer calls these two contrary effects the arithmetic and economic effect. The arithmetic effect is the increase of tax income with a hike. The economic effect is the before explained decline in demand and supply in labor and thereby, a decrease of income from labor taxes (Laffer 2004).

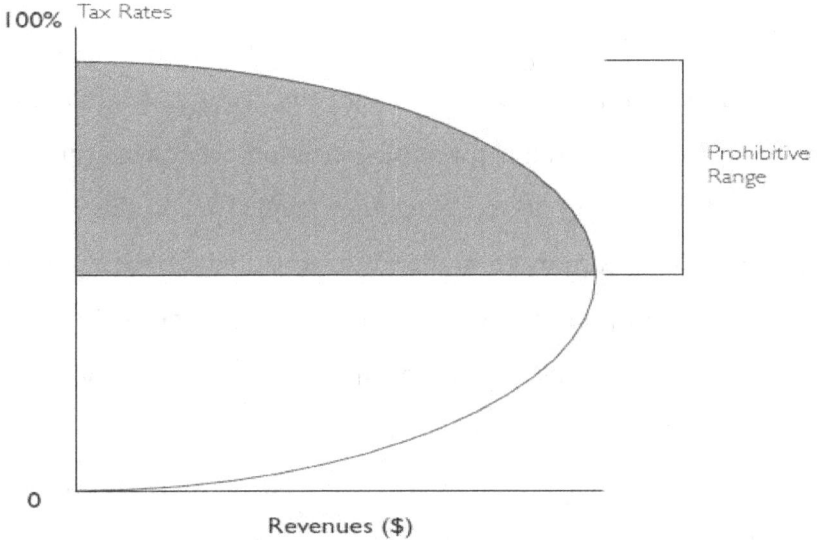

The Laffer Curve

Another effect, Laffer argues, is that declining tax rates can lead to an "incentive to increase output, employment and production" (Laffer 2004, S. 2). Furthermore, this kind of tax procedure helps to balance the budget because the so called tax cuts reduce the expenditures for demand-orientation i.e. unemployment sinks and the incomes increase (Laffer 2004). Hence, raise or decline of tax rates can help to a higher (or lower) matching between employer and employee.

3.5 Mismatching

Education-job mismatching

Following the paper of Allen and Van der Velden, there are several forms of mismatching in terms of a required education and the actually own education level. Based on other studies, Allen and Van der Velden observed that individuals who work in a position which needs less education, become on the one hand lower wages than individuals with the same level of education who work in position with an appropriate required education level. But on the other hand these individuals earn more in their overeducated job than individuals who have an appropriate education level for the certain job.

Furthermore, individuals who are undereducated, i.e. work in a job which needs a higher level of education than the certain person has, earns more than persons with the same level of education in an appropriate education level job. However, the certain individual has a lower wage than persons who also work in the undereducated job but have an appropriate level of education (Duncan and Hoffman 1982, Hartog and Oosterbeek 1988, Hersch 1991, Sicherman 1991, Cohn and Khan 1995, Van der Velden and Van Smoorenburg 1997, Allen and Van der Velden 2001).

All in all, Allen and Van der Velden and others observed that individuals who work in position with a lower needed education earn more than their colleagues for the job but less than their educational level could get out of them. If one compares the terms overeducation and undereducation, one can observes a stronger wage rate effect for the first one.

Thereby, overeducation respectively undereducation can have positive and negative effects. Whereas overeducation could harm the productivity of an employee, undereducation can raise the level of working of a person. Allen and Van der Velden explain this as follows: Individuals, who are in jobs where they are overeducated, feel their positions like a limitation of the utilisation of their skills. This is resulting in a loss of productivity and hence to a lower wage. Allen and Van der Velden call this the ceiling of productivity of a person. However, working in a job which is "too high" for an individual can raise the wage rate for this person. These jobs raise the productivity ceiling. Thus, employees can be more productive than in their normally position. Here, the productivity ceiling is determined by the own abilities of the individual. Persons in jobs which are normally "above" them try to do their best to fulfil the requirements of this position and to use the chance. Thereby, the wage rate difference in undereducated jobs is higher than in overeducated jobs.

Following the assignment theory, this situation leads to an allocation of workers in top-down form, dependent from their skills and the appropriate possible job. The best educated respectively skilled worker gets the most complex job. This goes down until the persons with no skills become a job with no requirements.

According to other theories, over- and undereducation can also be the result of imperfect information (Hartog 2000, Allen and Van der

Velden 2001). An example therefore can be seen in the bridge between school and work, where persons are mostly overeducated for their later first job.

In the end, van Ophem comes to the conclusion that present wages and non-wage job characteristics influence as well the search decisions of employees as future wages and non-wage job characteristics. These results are far away from "many empirical (and theoretical) investigations of search theory" (Van Ophem 1991, S. 151). This is the case because many empirical and theoretical search theory issues do not take the future wages and the non-wage job characteristics into account. Van Ophem argues that the search decision of an individual is highly dependent from the economic situation. The only way in poor labor market situation might be a promotion of the employee. The certain labor market position can be improved by this way.

Skill-job mismatching

Similar to the mismatching in educational-job form is the one of skill and job. However, the difference is that individuals in skill-job mismatching are already in work and search in many cases for another job after unemployment. Thereby, an over- or underqualification of the person considering the requirements of the new work is possible. Skill-job mismatching can lead to a significant welfare lost of a certain state in case of overqualification of the persons in their new jobs.

The Organization for Economic Co-operation and Development (OECD) has published on their website the theme of skills mismatch within a "hot issue" column (OECD 2005). For the OECD, skill mismatch is a very serious theme. Both, over- and under-skilling can lead to problems. In case of over-skilling, the available skills get lost and the expended resources to gain these skills were useless. Furthermore, worker who are over-skilled earn less than the one who are in jobs which require their abilities. Finally, these workers tend to be less satisfied.

The other case, the one of under-skilled workers, can for the OECD also lead to failures. With these kind of workers, firms "slow the rate at which more efficient technologies and approaches to work can be adopted" (OECD 2005, S. 1).

Some policies shall stop this behaviour. Especially small and medium-sized enterprises (SMEs) have to identify what effective work is and how the organizational practises work. Therefore, the SMEs have to make the best out of their existing skill pool with promoting innovations and transfer technologies and practises who match with their workforces.

The side of employees can further educates and trains their skills, even when they are out of school respectively university. This helps especially in the case of under-skilling. Furthermore, more transparent information about hiring positions can reduce under-skilling, too. This fact can be seen as well on the side of employees as on the one of employers. Potential new workers can better see whether a position is the right for them or not. Employers can take a closer look at potential new workers when they truly show not only their education level but also their available skills.

Following the OECD, most of the analysis of mismatch concentrates rather on qualification than skills because the former has a wider data base available. Therefore, the "Programme for the International Adult Assessment of Adult Competencies" (PIAAC) was implemented. The PIAAC measures as well the skills as the use of those.

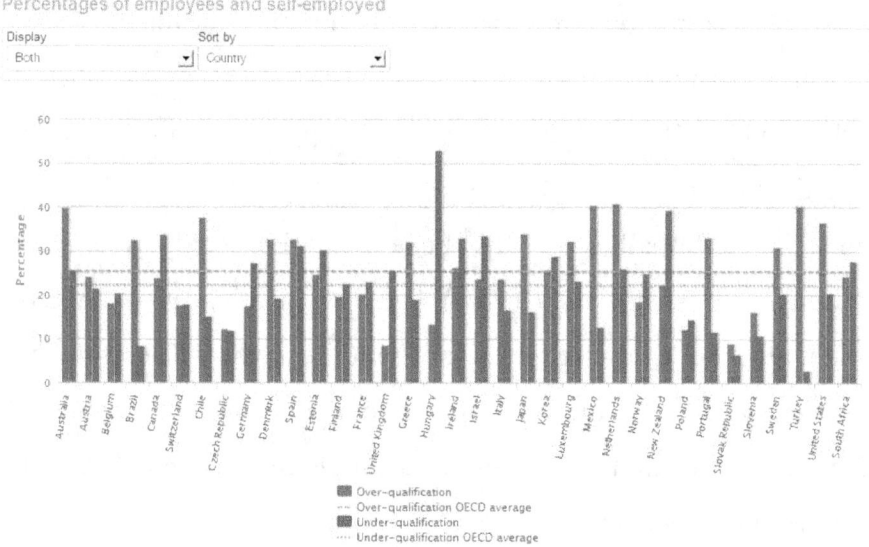

Considering the financial crisis in the US, the Federal Reserve Bank of Chicago published an article with the question if there is a skill mismatch in the US labor market(Faberman and Mazumder 2012). Within this article, the two authors explain what a skill mismatch is and furthermore which theories assume which results. They argue that skill mismatch is a great problem because on the one hand "it is harder for job seekers to find a suitable work" and on the other hand "it is harder for employers to find qualified applicants" (Faberman and Mazumder 2012, S. 1). Amongst others, the Federal Reserve Bank observed the situation of the US labor market from 2007 to 2011. Result is that some groups of employers are now with a higher degree unemployed while others have more job vacancies and hence a lower unemployment rate. Namely, the individuals with the "lowest" and "highest" skills have in consequence of the financial crisis first a higher unemployment rate and later, in 2011, a rate which is similar to the one of the before-crisis time. By contrast, the "medium" skills persons suffers like the other two groups, but in the post-crisis US labor market situation, their unemployment rate is significantly higher.

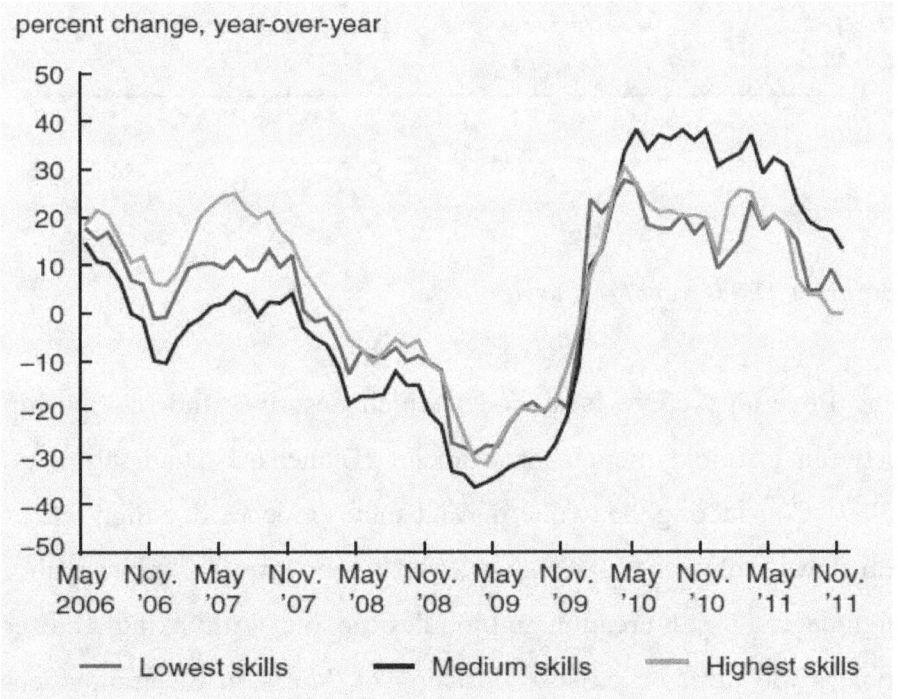

Faberman and Mazumder explain these arguments with the help of the Beverage curve. Furthermore, they show this curve for the US labor market.

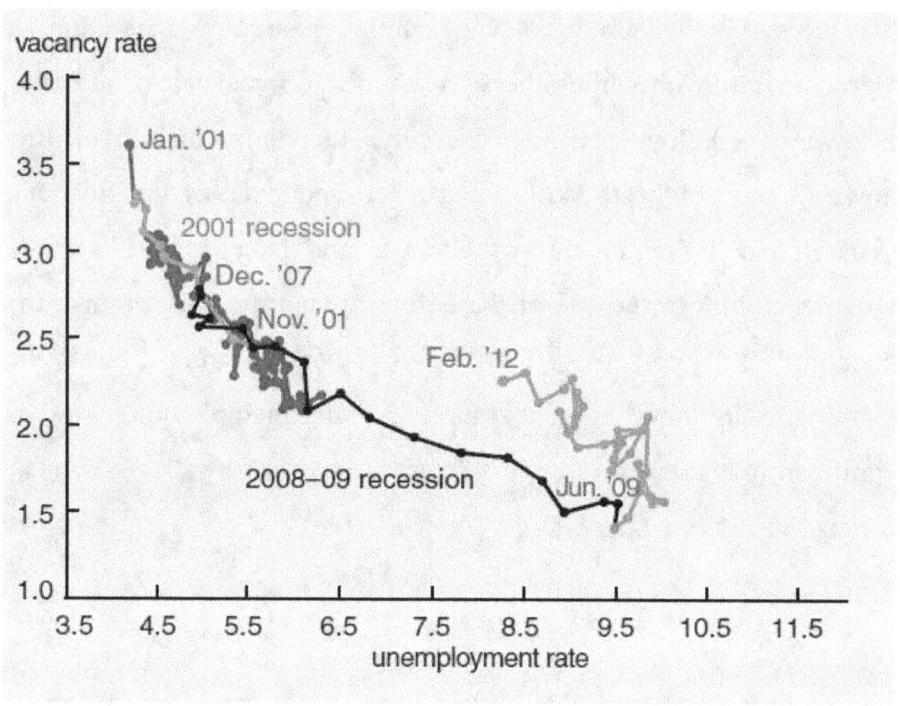

Excurse: The Beveridge Curve

The Beveridge curve is a model which describes the relationship between unemployment and vacancies (Blanchard, Diamond et al. 1989). Considering the two terms and some evidence of a high rate of job flows within the US labor market, these flows are relate with a high degree of job creation and job destruction. With taking a closer look, a job turnover exists, consisting of "the sum of employment increases in new or expanding establishments and employment decreases in shrinking or dying establishments" (Blanchard, Diamond et al. 1989, S. 1, Davis and Haltiwanger 1991). With these large flows, the existing of unfilled jobs is as well possible as the existing of unemployed workers. Within their paper, Blanchard, Diamond et al. create a matching function which aggregates the relationships between the terms unemployment, vacancies and new hires.

Excurse: Polarization

According to the hypothesis of over- and underqualification and resulting mismatching in the labor market, Rohrbach-Schmidt and Tiemann give an approach called polarization. The focus of polarization is not that individuals are over- or underqualified but that the existing middle skilled jobs becomes less and less. Reason for this is the so called "computerization". Since the 1990s, there are more high and low skilled jobs originated than middle skilled jobs. On the one hand there are routine tasks, which can be accomplished by low skilled workers. On the other hand, some "analytic and interactive non-routine job tasks" exist, which can only performed by high skilled individuals. This middle skilled class is more and more done by computers. Exceptions thereby are jobs where computerization is not (fully) includable like truck driving or cleaning. The demand in such job profiles "is assumed to be increasing as well" (Rohrbach-Schmidt and Tiemann 2011, S. 41).

3.6 Relative Deprivation Theory

Income in comparison to job satisfaction is well developed by some researchers. But in this context, income mostly has been seen as absolute income. The question is not always "Am I happier with more money" but rather "Am I happier if I become more money than my colleagues". The comparison of job satisfaction and such questions is the base for the so called relative deprivation theory.

Within their paper, Clark and Oswald define two equations(Clark, Oswald et al. 1996). There is a standard economic utility equation for utility in the context of income and working

$$u = u(y,h,i,j)$$

with y as income, h as hours of work, i as set of individual parameters and j as set of job parameters. The second equation is one which will be finding rather in social psychology textbooks. Thereby, another term is included in the equation (8)

$$u = u(y,y^*,h,i,j)$$

where the term y^* stands for descriptions like deprivation, envy, jealousy or inequity (Clark and Oswald 1996). Hence, the second equation describes not only monetary measurable factors or factors of exactly numerical characterization. The additional term y* is a non-pecuniary one and it is not in all cases exactly measurable.

To measure job satisfaction in the context of the relative deprivation theory, the equation of "total" utility is implemented. This form is a psychological one and is mostly characterized as a "life satisfaction" function. One can write this equation as

$$v = v(u(y, h, \underline{i}, \underline{j}), \mu)$$

Where term u is the work utility with the terms income (y), number of hours of work (h), person-related characterizations ($\underline{i}$) and job-related characterizations ($\underline{j}$). The last missing term, µ, represents another form of utility. Psychologists determine this term for factors like "quality of family life, friendships, the individual's health, and many personal variables outside the realm of the economist" (Clark and Oswald 1996, S. 7).

Main results of the study of Clark and Oswald are two conclusions. First, the certain satisfaction level of a worker is negatively related in comparison to his or her earning level. Second, given a constant income, the level of satisfaction does decline with the level of education. Clark and Oswald argues that this might be because higher education includes higher aspiration in well paid jobs, but they also say that is no guaranteed right interpretation.

All in all, Clark and Oswald think that against economics textbooks, "comparisons in the utility function seem to matter" (Clark and Oswald 1996, S. 15). Growth can not be seen longer as a clear way to increases happiness. Hence, "the standard optimality results of the free market may fail to hold" (Clark and Oswald 1996, S. 15).

It seems that pecuniary aspects are just one important side of the matching terms in the labor market. Given this last citation, a closer look to non-pecuniary aspects has to be taken.

4 Non-pecuniary Aspects

4.1 Organizational view/employer's view

4.1.1 Recruitment & image of firms as an incentive for workers

Finding and hiring new good skilled, motivated and hardworking personal has his price. This kind of worker is rare and the real costs as well as the opportunity costs are high. During the hiring process, an organization respectively firm can not search for other personal. More precisely, if a firm start a hiring process with a certain individual, there is always another individual who can not observed furthermore. Firms try to avoid hiring persons who are in the end the poorer choice.

An instrument of firms to attract new good personal can be on the one hand the image of a certain firm. On the other hand firms can use special recruitment programs to find the best persons for a job.

With taking a look at the second term first, there are some facts who underline the importance of the recruitment of applicants. Following Rynes et al., one of three applicants decide to work for a special company because of the recruiter. So, the recruiter as a person is an important factor in hiring new personal. Otherwise, things like delays in recruitment phases have negative effects on the pool of possible applicants (Rynes, Bretz et al. 1991). Researches in this field disperse. While older research suggest, that recruitment measures have little influences on the decision of applicants for a firm or another, younger literature asserts the contrary view.

The other term, image, is rather the reversal of the process of searching for workers. In the recruitment process the firm is rather the active part, who search and bind persons. Image of firms on the other hand are more an argument for possible workers to apply themselves at certain organizations. A positive image can tip the balance for an applicant.

Friendship as a method of recruitment

Following Sterling, organizational recruitment is based with a significantly degree on friendships between worker and applicant (Sterling 2014). So called employee networks exist especially in markets with non-sequential job search. Here, organizations offer jobs and recruit candidates earlier. Furthermore, the certain firm try to recruit new employees rather in a segment where the certain applicant has already one or more friend(s) in the firm. Hence, applicants have an advantage if they are friends of already in the firm working persons. Thus, it is more likely that individuals in the non-sequential search market receive offers from hiring firms if they have such friends than if they have not. This leads to an interesting effect. Even if a candidate has rather lower-quality in the hiring process, the existing of a social network with currently employees of the firm increases the chance of getting hired (Fernandez, Castilla et al. 2000, Castilla 2005, Sterling 2014). Sterling assumes that organizations use this type of information gaining rather in markets, where this information is not directly available. This implies that networks have an important position in these markets. An effect of this procedure is that organizations tend to be "social capitalists" and try to "gain strategic human resource advantages" (Sterling 2014, S. 2350). Normally, on markets where information about the quality of applicant is fully available, social networks should be largely redundant and hence should not affect the likelihood of offering jobs to certain candidates (Fernandez, Castilla et al. 2000, Sterling 2014). However, in labor market with more non-sequentially job search behaviour of candidates, organizations offer vacancies more often to individuals with friends in the firm. This effect is even stronger if the candidate works outside of the home educational institution.

Following Sterling, this approach has beside the incomplete information argument another significantly advantage for the organization. Individuals who have friends in the organization and get hired by this firm tend less often to quit the job - as a difference to persons who get hired and have before the hiring no friends in the firm.

These findings may have be a kind of racism. Similar to forms of racism like gender or skin colour in job advertisements and generally in the searching for new workers, hiring new workers on the base of friendships could be a form of racism.

Sterling argues that friendship-hiring can exclude a part of possible worker or applicant, respectively. Those persons who have no friends in the organization have a significant disadvantage towards the ones who have friendships within the firm. This could lead to inequality of income within the population. Organizations are a mayor source of income for most of the individuals.

Following the approach of employee referrals, another paper has to be mentioned. Fernandez, Castilla and Moore observed the factor of referrals by already employed workers for the hiring process by employers (Fernandez, Castilla et al. 2000). Within this observation, they try to show the so called turnover of a certain applicant, i.e. the investment of the firm in the applicant after his hiring. Fernandez, Castilla and More have focused their work on the demand side of the job-person matching process. So, the organizational view of costs and gains of a hiring. The existing of social networks is of crucial importance for applicants as well as for employers. Following the employee referral approach, current members of the certain organization make their suggestions with their employer considering new employees. Hence, they are include in the decision making process of their enterprise. Based on this procedure, Fernandez, Castilla and Moore present three "competing explanations of the referral hiring process" (Fernandez, Castilla et al. 2000, S. 1289). Namely,

1.) richer pool
2.) better match
3.) social enrichment.

Furthermore, they show five mechanisms which work within these explanations.

a) expansion of the pool of applicants by referrals
b) tendency for people to refer others like themselves
c) reputation protection
d) information advantages of hiring via referrals
e) social processes that occur post hire.

Whereas mechanism a, b and c can be included into explanation 1, mechanism d belongs to explanation 2 and mechanism e to explanation 3.

Mechanism a, the expansion of the pool applicants by referrals, is an approach where organizations trust employee referrals to stretch the amount of possible new workers. In addition, the certain firm might find applicants which it has not taken into account without the employee referral.

Mechanism b, the tendency for people to refer others like themselves, is based on the homophilous theory (Granovetter 1995). Individuals tend to have social ties with others who are similar to themselves. This can be very helpful for the hiring process because the social aspect of individuals is for employers a so called "black box". They do not know if the, for example, characteristics of an applicant fit to the organization. With the concept of social ties and employee referrals by (for the firm suitable) workers, the certain organization can distinguish better between referred and non-referred applicants.

Mechanism c, the reputation protection argument, explain the fact that workers who give employee referrals do not want to harm themselves if the referred applicant gets hired and then is not suitable for the firm. Based on this argumentation, employee referrals should maintain the firm standard of workers - if it not even rises. Already badly workers do not give employee referrals because they do not want to worsen their own situation if the hired worker is not good at his job. Hence, only the good and moderate individuals should suggest new persons.

Mechanism a, b and c can be pooled into the explanation of a richer pool. This approach suggests that the "referred applicants should be more qualified and more readily hireable than nonreferral applicants" (Fernandez, Castilla et al. 2000). Furthermore has the pool of possible new workers a higher amount of candidates. Employers can use the capabilities of employees by recruiting new individuals. Hence, the organization uses the social capital of their workers to generate new possible investments, gets a higher turnover with the hired persons and also improves the future social capital.

In addition to the explanation of the richer pool, the explanations of better match and social enrichment have to be considered. The better match approach is based on mechanism d - information advantages of hiring via referrals. The idea behind this assumption is thinkable like a circle. Social ties between the currently in the firm working person and the applicant is as well existing as the information connection between the worker and the employer. Hence, the desire of the organization is now that hires based on employee referrals increase the information about the new worker for the hiring organization. So called "hard-to-measure" information like characteristics or personal behaviour might be better seen with this relation. On the side of the applicants, this relation has another advantage. With getting more information from the firm, especially hardly available information from inside, the applicant knows better "what they are getting into" (Fernandez, Castilla et al. 2000, S. 1293). On employment side, information gathering happens through two ways. On the one side, there is the relatively indirect method of gaining information about the applicant. Employers compare the applicants with the persons who give the employee referral. Because of the theory of homophily principle (see mechanism b), a comparison is easy. The second method is direct information gathering. Here, the employer just asks "the referrer about characteristics of the referral candidate" (Fernandez, Castilla et al. 2000, S. 1295).

Finally, explanation three, the social enrichment approach, is based on mechanism e (social processes that occur after hiring). Within this assumption, referrer and referral bonds an aiding relation, like a mentoring program. In contrast to the better match approach where the actors are socially isolated, in the social enrichment model actors help each other. Thus, this approach has rather social goals in form of commonly better matching by social interaction for the employer. In the better match approach, isolated actors are admittedly paid for example for good referrals, albeit there is no social interaction after a hiring in form of mentoring.

However, social enrichment can also have negative properties. Information exchange and mentoring programs between the workers can work against the employer. An example therefore is the study of Blau (Blau 1985). He tested the social interacting between nurses. As a result he has shown that there is a "tendency for nurse's friends to cover for one another" (Blau 1985, Fernandez, Castilla et al. 2000, S. 1297). Following another study of Bailey and Waldinger, there are also negative aspects for new workers in the social enrichment theory. In this study, workers do not help new hired persons if they do not know them already. Just in case of an existing friendship before the hiring, the workers support the new ones with on-the-job training (Bailey and Waldinger 1991, Fernandez, Castilla et al. 2000). Thus, social capital also involves some kind of risk. But all in all, a deep relationship between referral and referrer after the hiring in form of for example a mentoring program affects the tie of the new worker and the organization.

For Bridges and Villemez, social ties between individuals in the context of work relations exist, however there are rather a "by-product of successful long-term participation in the labor market" (Bridges and Villemez 1986). This can be especially seen in the weak ties term. In addition, weak ties in the labor market or labor market contacts, respectively, are "nearly universal" and furthermore "enjoyed by a variety of socio-demographic groups" (Bridges and Villemez 1986, S. 579). Bridges and Villemez think that the term of strong/weak ties is not the only and not even the most important of person related relationships within the labor market. All in all, strong and weak ties are not of crucial importance and available for the entire employed population and not for some special groups of individuals.

4.1.2 Coercion/slavery

Following Acemoglu and Wolitzky, one possibility to navigate the effort of workers is the application of coercion (Acemoglu and Wolitzky 2011). Coercion, or in the harder variety slavery, can increase the effort of workers. There are two basic assumptions of the coercion model. First, the worker has in these circumstances no wealth which leads to a limited liability constraint. The principal or organization, respectively, can punish or reward the worker as he wants. Second, a so called reservation utility of the worker changes - depended from the amount of "guns" or coercion the principal chooses. This second assumption is for Acemoglu and Wolitzky of crucial importance for the model, because the named "coercion is mainly about forcing workers to accept employment, or terms of employment, that they would otherwise reject" (Acemoglu and Wolitzky 2011, S. 2).
In Acemoglu's and Wolitzky's model, the labor market is signed by the factors scarcity of labor, coercion, effort and the so called outside options.

This model is designed as a principal-agent-problem with the employers as the principal and the workers as agents. The employers can not control the effort of the workers except they increase or decrease the exerted effort. Thus, coercion and effort of the workers are complements. The workers on the other side reduce their effort until the coercion becomes a higher level. Acemoglu and Wolitzky found out that lower outside options for the workers are coerced more and lead to a higher degree of effort in equilibrium. Hence, coercion can prevent the employer from paying too high wages because he can ex ante increase the degree of coercion which leads to an increase in effort and an equilibrium - without paying higher wages. Result of this is that employers who are more "productive" will use higher coercion levels. Following Acemoglu and Wolitzky, employees will be worse off if they match with such more productive employers. All in all, workers who worked for more productive employers "receive high expected monetary compensation, despite having low welfare" (Acemoglu and Wolitzky 2011). In addition, in the argumentation of Acemoglu and Wolitzky, coercion always disembogues in a "socially inefficient" status because resources of the workers, namely utility, flow in costly ways to the employer.

Each of the two factors of this model, scarcity of labor and outside options create an effect - the labor demand effect and the outside options effect. Both can change the level of effort and coercion with increase or decrease. The labor demand effect implies that the price of a good of a certain employer is dependent from the production decisions of all other employers. Hence, if the demand for labor is high, the level of coercion and effort of the certain worker is high, too. This leads to increased productivity and thus to a high amount of products which results in low prices for the good. The reverse case eventuates if the demand for labor is low. The employers have to attract the workers with low levels of coercion or effort, respectively, which lead to a lower productivity, lower outcomes of goods and a higher price for the certain good.

As a second effect, the outside option effect exists. This effects work against the labor demand effect. Outside options are other possible employers for the certain worker. If the level of coercion in his current firm gets too high, the certain worker changes the employer to become a lower coercion degree. By this argumentation, a surplus of labor results in higher coercion and hence in job changes of workers to employers with lower coercion levels.

Extensions of the Coercion Model

Acemoglu and Wolitzky implement some extensions in their model of coercion of employers. The first one is the introduction of ex ante investments. With this extension, Acemoglu and Wolitzky show that workers try to underinvest in their productivity skills to "holdup" the level of coercion of the employer. In addition, the workers overinvest in skills regarding the improvement of outside options. Following this extension, Acemoglu and Wolitzky suggest that this can be "a potential explanation for why coercion is particularly prevalent in effort-intensive low-skill labor, and relatively rare in activities that require investment in relationship-specific skills or are "car-intensive" (Fenoaltea 1984, Acemoglu and Wolitzky 2011, S. 3).

As a second extension, coercion can be seen as a method that affects also the interim outside options of the certain worker and furthermore influence them if ex post coercion is costly. Third, Acemoglu and Wolitzky include a variant where punishment choices are made before the matching between worker and employer applies. Thereby, an economies of scale effect leads to greater labor abundance. Result of this is that coercion is now more profitable for productive or extractive, respectively, institutions. As a last extension, a "trading in slaves" model is implemented where employers can trade with other employers and sell or buy workers. Not surprisingly, this trade reduces the welfare of a certain agent. In addition, the social welfare of workers might sink, too. This follows from a higher productivity and thus a higher level of coercion of the certain principal from trading workers.

4.1.3 Labor Market Matching and Racial Harassment

Some factors influence the matching between employee and employer in the context of the labor market. Thereby, different stages can be observed - a pre-hired stage of employees, a stage where an employee is be in the payroll and may search for a better job (on-the-job search) and finally the quitting of the current job for another or for unemployment.

Racial harassment can thereby occur in every stage of this cycle. In a paper of Bertrand and Mullainathan, the pre-stage of this problem was observed. In conclusion, racial harassment is a hampering factor in hiring new workers. Further papers, like a study of Shields and Price, concentrate on racial harassment within a certain job. Shields and Price underline this with an example of British nurses who are members of ethnic minorities (Shields and Price 2002) (for empirical evidence see 5.2).

Bertrand and Mullainathan answer in their paper on ads in newspapers of Chicago and Boston for job applications (Bertrand and Mullainathan 2003). Within this study, they answer with very White and very African-American sounding names. The study shows a significant discrimination for African-American names and therefore a disadvantage for individuals with such names. Concrete have the African-American sounding names send about 15 resumes to get one callback. In comparison to the White sounding names, this is a 50 percent higher effort (about 10 resumes for one callback). Bertrand and Mullainathan find out even more about discrimination relate to matching in labor market. Another disadvantage for African-American sounding names is given in the fact that a certain resume has to be a better quality than one by a White sounding name to ensure equal premises for a certain job application. However, improved credentials do not alleviate fears of potential employers. Hence, for Bertrand and Mullainathan, African-Americans have beside the disadvantages of finding a job another border in form of the constraint to have better qualifications.

The occurrence of discrimination is thereby given in every kind of hiring firm. Even for great firms with guidelines state by the status of an "Equal Opportunity Employer", discrimination was observed. Furthermore, federal contractors with affirmative action laws have not a less discrimination level than other employers. Bertrand and Mullainathan conclude, that "discrimination levels are statistically indistinguishable across all the occupation and industry categories".

4.2 Workers/employee's view

4.2.1 Job satisfaction

An important aspect of job searching is job satisfaction. Thereby, job satisfaction is highly dependent on the terms job search and job changes. Some determinants lead to a high degree of job satisfaction. Relations to colleagues and supervisors as well as different tasks in the current job and job security are relevant for satisfaction (Cornelißen 2009). With lower satisfaction, the chance of searching for another work increases and the chance of change becomes a higher possibility. Kristensen and Westergård-Nielsen agree with this argument in a study of Danish families from 1994 to 2000 (Kristensen and Westergård-Nielsen 2004).
Following Warr, the term job satisfaction can be separated into ten features (Kahneman, Diener et al. 1999, Warr 1999). Theses features are personal control, opportunity for skill-use, job demands, variety, environmental clarity, income, physical security, supportive

supervision, interpersonal control and values social position. Cornelißen uses these features in the context of data from Germany to observe which of them are more important than the others (Cornelißen 2009) (for empirical evidence see 5.2). Kristensen and Westergård-Nielsen found differences between these features. While satisfaction for Danish people is the most important factor of a job, they argue that in another study for individuals in the UK, the term of security of a current job is the leading fact (Ward and Sloane 2000). Kristensen and Westergård-Nielsen explain this with a different social welfare system in Denmark and the UK. Danish people do not have such a fear of being unemployed, because the state pays in this case more than in the UK. Furthermore, Denmark is one of the leading countries in a study, who includes a table of the most "satisfied countries", which correlates with the fact that Danish people quit their job more often if it is not satisfying (Yusuf 2009).

Satisfaction with life
Denmark
Switzerland
Austria
Iceland
Australia
Finland
Sweden
Canada
Ireland
Luxembourg
Norway
Netherlands

For Kristensen and Westergård-Nielsen an explanation of job satisfaction could also be the *rate* of unemployment. They show in their Danish example, that a higher unemployment rate decrease job dissatisfaction. This could be explained with outside options.

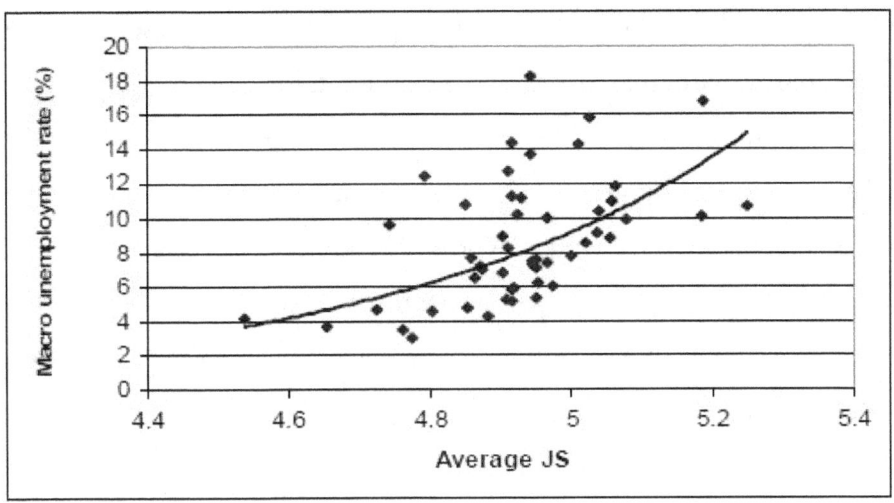

If more people are unemployed, jobs in the market are rare. So, with fewer options to switch the job, individuals are more satisfied to have the currently one.

A similar approach is raised by Böckerman and Ilmakunnas. They observed possible job disamenities and their results in job satisfaction and on-the-job search. Therefore, Böckerman and Ilmakunnas take a look at the Finnish labor market under the condition of "adverse working conditions" at the workplace. They find out, that workers are more willing to switch their jobs or even quit and stop working if there is a high degree of adverse working conditions. Furthermore, this kind of workers search more often for new possible jobs, for instance via on-the-job search. Böckerman and Ilmakunnas argue that workers become an amount of compensation in terms of wage rate to equal the adverse working conditions. But if the compensation is not high enough, switching the job is the better alternative because this can increase the utility. The Finnish labor market thereby is already a pioneer in paying pecuniary compensations for adverse working conditions. Binding contracts in Finland contain such compensations. But it seems that the jobs are more heterogeneous (and so the different work requirements) than money can equal.

However, although adverse working conditions are substantially factors for increase job dissatisfaction, compensating such working conditions only have a minor (positive) effect on job satisfaction (Böckerman and Ilmakunnas 2004).

4.2.2 Quit intentions

Gender

In his paper, Viscusi tries to make a difference between the quit behaviour of men and women (Viscusi 1980). Although Viscusi deny such behaviour in an earlier study from 1979, he argues that there are some aspects as well in the organizational/firm view as in the workers view which lead to quicker quits of women than men. From the point of view of a female worker, an important aspect is a quit in consequence of a change of the location of the husband's job. In this case, wives quit their jobs because they are in a co-working status, i.e. wives are more or less secondary earners. The man is the main earner and the woman's job is some kind of additional income.

Furthermore, Viscusi argues that the working time period is for women some kind of gaining experiences. If this time period is over, women often quit their jobs.

In the context of organizational view, there are also some arguments by Viscusi. For him, "the greater rate of job leavers (quits) among females also contributes to the discrepancy in unemployment rates" (Viscusi 1980, S. 389). In addition, in a special case, where women and men are equal in absolute quitting levels, the optimizing firm would pay less to women than to men. The reason for this behaviour is the less responsiveness of women to additional wage payments. Men, who look for more utilizing jobs in terms of a higher payoff have to be held by the currently employer. Hence, firms have to pay a higher compensation for the effort of men than for the effort of women because women are not as career-minded as men are.

Notwithstanding these factors of different wage rates and quit behaviours have a true core, some aspects are outdated. In modern times, women are no more the co-worker respectively co-earner for their husband. With a greater labor market entry, the gap between men and women earner becomes smaller and smaller. Even in the paper of Viscusi from 1980, he observes a decline in quitting jobs by women in the manufacturing industries from 80% (women quit 80% oftener their job than men) in 1958 to 16% in 1968.

Another different approaches were given by Hodson (Hodson 1989). A central question is what makes women satisfied with their jobs and why there is a difference between women and men. Hodson tries to give two explanations. First, women just have a higher satisfaction with their work because they use different comparison groups. The second approach is that men in contrary to women explain dissatisfaction automatically with a bad job. This could be the case because men have other socializations than women. More or less, one might conclude that men and women have different job satisfactions because men define them more with their work. This might come from the fact that men are in past in most cases the main earner and if their work is not fulfilling, they feel bad.

Age

One possible factor of different job satisfaction can be the age of the employee. Clark, Oswald and Warr present a study which support earlier workings in the fact that job satisfaction in relation to the age of the individual is a U-shaped curve. Furthermore, the effect of age seems to have a larger influence than gender, education, ethnic background or income (Clark and Oswald 1996, Clark 1997).
With entering the labor market, a person is on a well-motivated level. Following Clark, Oswald and Warr, this motivation, respectively job satisfaction, sinks from then until the late twenties or early thirties and finally increases continually till the retirement (Herzberg and Mausner 1957, Clark, Oswald et al. 1996). With some experience in a certain job, a young employee feels a continually increasing boredom. Furthermore, with every year of working, possible opportunities decline, which can lead to a higher dissatisfaction. By utilizing upcoming possibilities which come from things like

increased skills with time, individuals can get a higher job satisfaction in the following years.

Clark, Oswald and Warr published some other studies, where the young group is not as satisfied as above-mentioned. In a paper of Quinn and Staines from 1979, these individuals tend be more dissatisfied than the older group (Quinn and Staines 1979). So, the U-shaped job satisfaction curve could start at a lower point, sinks until about year 30 and increase above the beginning point until retirement has reached.

Further views have been carried together by Lee and Wilbur (Lee and Wilbur 1985). Beside the above-mentioned U-shaped function, there are two other relationships between age and job satisfaction. First, a simple positive and initially increase in satisfaction relates to an increase in age (Hulin and Smith 1965). Hence, there is no decline in a certain part of life in job satisfaction. The second theory is again a positive and linear increase in job satisfaction - until a point where a terminal period begins which result in a significant decline in satisfaction with the certain job (Saleh and Otis 1964, Carrell and Elbert 1974).

But why might the old employees be the most satisfied ones in the most common cases? Clark, Oswald and Warr try to explain this with some arguments. For instance, older people have more desirable characteristics than young ones. They also have a higher intrinsic job satisfaction. Furthermore, older ones have specific work values. Experiences, which can be achieve with time is an advantage in relation to get jobs with high requirements. This, older individual rather become such jobs, which are mostly more satisfying than jobs with low requirements. Finally, the old ones might just lower their expectations of a job. Young people, who start their career mostly have ideals of a perfect job and try to find such one. With time, the expectations of the individual become more realistic and approach with the job circumstances.

Socio-cultural Background

The thesis in this context is that individuals from certain regions of the world have a higher chance to get hired by firms than other under the ceteris paribus condition. A field experiment from Bertrand and Mullainathan compares typical white and black names and their influences on call-backs in order to find a job through an interview. Bertrand and Mullainathan found out that white names have to send about ten resumes to become one call-back and so one interview for a job offer. Black names, by contrast, have to send about 15 call-backs. Following Bertrand and Mullainathan, this gap of 50% can be equalised with an eight-year-experience advance in a certain job (Bertrand and Mullainathan 2003).

The statistics speak for themselves: "Compared to Whites, African Americans are twice as likely to be unemployed and earn nearly 25 percent less when they are employed" (Bertrand and Mullainathan 2003, S. 2). But there are different opinions. Some argue that there are race signals and that these signals lower the productivity. Another meaning is that through profit-maximization the best-possible worker becomes the job. Hence, discrimination is no more a factor. Finally, a "reverse discrimination" can be observed - if two candidates contest for the same job and if one is for instance a White American and one a African American, the employer decides to hire the African American (Bertrand and Mullainathan 2003).

In a British study, Shields and Price observed the influences of racial harassment on nurses who are members of an ethnic minority and how these impacts affect the job satisfaction and quit behaviour of them. They search in this particular case for two forms of racial harassment: on the one hand harassment from work colleagues (employee discrimination) and on the other hand harassment from patients (consumer discrimination). Shield and Price found that these ethnic minority nurses were discriminated about 40% from colleagues and with more than 64% from patients (Shields and Price 2002) (for empirical evidence see 5.2).

The result of racial harassment is a bad for both sides. On the one hand the job satisfaction of nurses decline with time and intensity of harassment. But beside these "mental costs" there are also social costs. Train a nurse-to-be is expansive. Shields and Price argue that the costs are about £50,000. The majority of these costs are to be borne by the taxpayer (Shields and Price 2002). If a new nurse now is to be afflicted with racial harassment, she becomes dissatisfaction with her profession. So, she quit her job and search for another or gets unemployed. In any case, the costs of her education are useless. Furthermore, Shields and Price say that these social costs are for young nurses the highest ones (Shields and Price 2002). With a certain age, a nurse grossed the costs. Hence, a fresh educated nurse who quit her job after a month of work is the worst case and has the highest social costs for the taxpayer.

Education

Job satisfaction is an important term, maybe even the most important one, in the job searching of individuals. With a higher education, better paid jobs can be achieved. Better paid jobs leads in most circumstances to a higher amount of money. Furthermore, better non-pecuniary aspects could be reached by persons with a higher educational degree like a college graduation. Here, one more time, the relative has to be seen, not the absolute. In absolute terms, a higher education leads to both, more money and more job satisfaction. But empirical evidence show that individuals who are better educated, need even more than a estimated advance in pecuniary as well as non-pecuniary aspects to be satisfied (Clark and Oswald 1996, Oshagbemi 1997).

4.2.3   Procrastination

The probability of searching a job, especially in the case of unemployment, is highly dependent from a factor, called procrastination. Procrastination means that possible present actions differ to a later point of time. Procrastination can be applicable onto the process of job searching. Especially for unemployed persons is this factor a bad attribute. Unemployed persons delay their job searching onto a later point of time over and over again. Results of this behaviour can be a less well-paid job or even no job at all.

In their paper, Lay and Brokenshire examine the factor of procrastination as well as the attribute conscientiousness and further so called "person-task characteristics" (Lay and Brokenshire 1997). Therefore, they levied a study about 32 unemployed males and 32 unemployed females and their behaviour in above-mentioned terms. Within the study, two times, t_1 and t_2, are observed. At t_1, "conscientiousness was positively related to each of the person-task characteristics and to intentions to engage in the composite of job-search activities; trait procrastination was not" (Lay and Brokenshire 1997, S. 83). However, in time t_2, which was two weeks later, "trait procrastination predicted self-reported job-search behaviour, controlling for initial intentions, with procrasting exhibiting less job-search activity in the two week interim, compared to nonprocrastinators" (Lay and Brokenshire 1997). Amongst others they find out, that procrastinators rather "view their tasks as more aversive, and themselves as less competent and more compelled, compared to nonprocrastinators" (Lay and Brokenshire 1997, S. 84). Hence, individuals who tend to have a higher procrastination level have also a higher probability to be for a longer time unemployed if they have once no job. This is an important fact for job searching, especially in the case of unemployment. With no job, individuals who procrastinate feel less self-confident. They delay the process of job searching for a later time and so become less self-assurance, feel less competent and so the procrastination circle increases. Lay and Brokenshire observed that unemployed persons who think that those job-search activities are less important and less pleasant and furthermore have a relatively low self-seen competence in this fields have also higher levels of procrastinatory behaviour within a two-week interval.

The probability of one's procrastination degree is modelled in a so called "goal-directed behaviour". Bagozzi choose three task characteristics to explain whether a person want to reach a goal or not (in procrastination sense). Therefore, the person first has to choose between some options which are available to her - here, some possible job activities. Now, the first person-task characteristic takes effect - the "perceived self-efficacy or perceives competence in carrying out each activity". The second one is the "perceived likelihood that each mean will lead to achievement of a goal or to performance of a target behaviour". The last person-task characteristic is the "perceived pleasantness or aversiveness of means" (Bagozzi 1992, Lay and Brokenshire, 1997, S. 87). With face up these questions about person-task characteristics, the procrastination level of one can be seen.

4.2.4   Social ties between individuals

The kind of tie between several individual is an important fact of the question how existing job offers can observe by certain persons.

Economic literature distinguishes between strong ties and weak ties. Both variants are crucial to find new, better paid and fulfilling jobs.

Strong ties

Communication respectively the contact between individuals can be distinguished in two ways - string ties and weak ties. Strong ties thereby represent individuals who have similar attributes. They are so called "homophilous" (Liu and Duff 1972, S. 361). These "communication relationships" are effective, because given knowledge of one can reach fast other individuals of the same attributes. So, "communication between source and receiver leads to greater homophily in knowledge, beliefs, and overt behavior" (Rogers and Bhowmik 1970, Liu and Duff 1972, S. 361). Furthermore, Rogers and Bhowmik argues that source and receiver should be homophilous in some variables and heterophilious in some other. The allocation of these aspects depends on the current situation.

But these homophilous relationships between individuals can also have some disadvantages. If close friends with mostly the same attributes relate within a circle of homophilous persons, the known information is always the same. For example, the given job offers which is known in a homophilous area is known by one (e.g. the source) who inform the others (the receivers). The information circulates amongst all individuals. Hence, all know the current job offers. However, other offers by not known firms can not observe. In the end, current job offers are either known by all individuals or by no one.

Another approach is considered by Sterling (Sterling 2014). Within her paper, she examines whether hiring a new worker is dependent from the fact, that these persons have friends in the certain firm. Thereby, social networks of individuals are very important. Organizations use the relationship of their currently worker to a potentially new one to get information. One problem of hiring new personal is the fact of incomplete respectively asymmetrical information. The potentially new worker knows all about her, for instance motivation, health status, soft skills etc. However, the organization can only become some respectively less qualified information about the hiring person. Therefore, actually workers, who are friends of the potentially new worker, can estimate the missing information. Following Granovetter or Marsden and Gorman, social networks lead to half of the acquisition of jobs and "as often as formal job search methods" (Granovetter 1995, Marsden and Gorman 2001, Sterling 2014, S. 2341).

This form of searching for appropriate candidates has another advantage. Every cycle of search for a candidate, become applications, conduct interviews, decide and become a rejection from the chosen one is costly. The time and effort of choosing a candidate who is not interested in the end is lost. So, organizations try to minimize this cost factor of missing information about the candidate with the help of social networks and friends with their ties to candidates. Within this problem, another one can be solved.

Organizations that search for candidates who decide finally against an employment in this organization lead also to a miss of the opportunity - make offers to candidates who might have joined the firm but have since found jobs elsewhere (Roth and Xing 1994, Kagel and Roth 2000).

Weak ties

To breach this circle of information, weak ties are the antidote. Weak ties to acquaintances offer new possibilities. Other information circles have other information. So, with weak ties, the border of homophilous, strong tie information circles can bridge. As a result, all individuals gain more information and so more job offers. Finally, the allocation of jobs is better and therefore pareto-optimality is a possibility.

Old boy network

Saloner observed the s called "old boy network" or respectively "old girl network" is the context of a hiring process (Saloner 1985). Employers search especially for skilled positions a third party who can give subjective personal opinions about applicant. So, low-quality workers can be screen out. This reduces the amount of costs of time and money. Furthermore, employees get deeper information about the applicant and especially about his or her skills. Incomplete information such as years of schooling and experiences, grades and so on are hence no more the only source of information (Saloner 1985, Simon and Warner 1992).

5   Discussion

Within the context of pecuniary and non-pecuniary job aspects of individuals, one can cherish, that pecuniary methods can easier shown than non-pecuniary. Especially the non-pecuniary factor of job satisfaction and its features (see. 4.2.1) are more or less subjective impressions of people. Furthermore, these subjective impressions can be different from individual to individual. So, a method to measure the influence of non-pecuniary aspects in job searching is difficult. Nonetheless, some papers show results for measuring such aspects, like job satisfaction.

Although non-pecuniary aspects in job searching, quitting and satisfaction measuring are controversial, it's an important part in finding out why people search a certain job. Given the upper papers and studies, it's maybe even the more important part compared to pecuniary aspects. Today's themes like work-life-balance, childcare in firms or flexible working hours and their importance in firm presentations and hiring interviews be at least indicative for these things.

What have to be targeted are the economy of a certain state in combination with its labor market and the facts of income and job satisfaction. Especially in a well developed state with high socio-economic standards is job satisfaction an important factor. The income is already in an above average status compared to all countries, the labor market is stabile as well as the state itself. Income plays further a role in the working process of an individual, but factors like job satisfaction may become more substance. As a contrary, workers of states like emerging nations may tend to focus more on the term income. The state is not as well stabile as some developed ones and jobs can be lost quite earlier. For instance, an organ of well developed counties and their labor market are unions for all great industry parts. Unions prevent workers from exploitation by employers and are an important factor in negotiations for higher wages. In emerging nations, unions may not have such a weighty position in the labor market than in well developed states. Furthermore, influences like corruption can hinder unions and their staffing from administer their office. Bribery of certain persons leads to failed union policy. Therefore, income is a key factor in working in not well developed states. With higher income, workers of union are for instance no longer so vulnerable for bribery and may be able to enforce higher wages. This can again lead to less vulnerability for bribery or similar influences. Now terms like job satisfaction become more importance than before. Income has further a high relevance but in comparison, it sinks.

5.1 Dependency of pecuniary and non-pecuniary aspects of individuals in the labor market

Following Becker's basic model of matching using the example of marriage, individuals always trying of become a gain with searching for higher partners. These result have to be discussed - not at least because such a matching version can not lead to market clearing. With searching for the best gain of a certain individual by marry another person, one person always lost. The more "good" individuals are matched with others, the less are in the market. This leads to a basement of persons who are no "good" matches. Even if the reasons for matching are no pecuniary ones, some individuals in the market might not have at least one good attribute to match for another one. Hence, these individuals will stand alone and have no match. Given the assumptions of Becker, these individuals are furthermore single households and have not the possibility to get the advantages of matching - and so stay in a worst position in the market.

Transferred to the context of labor market matching does that mean that there are some possible employees who do not have a match with employers because either the first or the last one have no good attributes which will make a match positive. For example, firms who would coerce employees to work for nothing by long hours in a hard work would have no advantage for every kind of worker. On the other side there can be possible employees who have no hard skills, soft skills and in other ways as well no advantages for firms to hire them. In this context one can compare this group of individuals with the so called "base unemployment" - persons who are not includable into the working population for reasons like above-mentioned or others like constant illness or aversion of these individuals for working.

Following this argumentation, one can ask the question whether a welfare state support a basement of unmatched individuals. In states where there is an insurance that individuals become a certain amount of money in case of unemployment, incentives to work could suffer. For instance, if unemployed individuals would only work for money and no other factors, they would only become incentives to work if offers have a payoff over the unemployment insurance. Therefore, one might argument that the existence of a welfare state is harmful for the matching of employer and employee in the labor market. Without insurance in case of unemployment, individuals have a higher intention to work to become money and to satisfy their basic needs thereby. In this context, the balance between pecuniary and non-pecuniary aspects for persons is clearly in favour of the pecuniary ones. Job satisfaction, motivation and so on play only a minor role if individuals have to work to have for instance something to eat. Following this argumentation, one might also argument that the working conditions in states like Bangladesh or India might be as badly as they are because the employees have to work to stay alive and not to die for hunger or thirst - indifferently how the non-pecuniary job aspects are. Considering this background, firms can pressure (together) the wages of labourers until the first ones can not keep working because of a missing of basic needs.

Meaningful aspects in labor market matching are the factors income and job satisfaction. Most of the other aspects depend on these two ones. Thereby, income represents the mostly influential pecuniary factor, while job satisfaction is the mostly influential non-pecuniary factor. Considering the certain country, relative job satisfaction seems to be even more important comparing to relative income. Some empirical evidence supports these findings, whereas most of them were realized in well developed states like the US or the UK labor market. In states with less average income or a not as high living standard as in industrial nations, income is also a heavy weight factor. In contrast, non-pecuniary aspects like job satisfaction seem to be not as important as pecuniary ones in these countries. The above-mentioned approach underlines this. Empirical evidences lack in the field of reporting on pecuniary and non-pecuniary factors in such countries comparing to evidences in well developed countries (especially the US or Great Britain, the Scandinavia countries and many of western and middle Europe ones).

Another point is procrastination. The more you need income for the basically things in your life, the less is the need of procrastinate and be further unemployed. This factor may be even higher in so called welfare states with terms like unemployment insurance. People of developing countries have not the choice to procrastinate and hence to not match with an employer. If they do so, their basic needs might not to be fulfilled. Thus, procrastination is a non-pecuniary matching problem of developed countries.

Matching in the labor market is in a large part a question of age. The age of an employee explains a lot about his or her suggestions of a job as well as his or her satisfaction within a certain work. In the study of Quinn and Staines as well as in some others, job satisfaction is shown like a U-shaped curve (Quinn and Staines 1979). In this curve, starting employees are far more motivated in the beginning of their career than at the age of about 30. After this low point, the job satisfaction begins slowly to increase until the end of working and the career. Thus, one could argue, labor market matching is easier with older workers. There are also some points that underline this argument. For instance, older persons do not have such idealistic visions about their career or their job. There is a more realistic view. Furthermore, adepter employees have in average more skills than younger ones. This fact is a result of the gain in experience over years. With more and more working years, individuals become hard skills on the one hand, i.e. physical or mental abilities for the certain job. On the other hand, persons gain with more experience also in the soft skill area. So, they are for example more self-confidant or have a better empathy in conversation with colleagues and supervisors. Both skill types are with a high degree the result of working years, experience and age. Furthermore, both types lead to a higher satisfaction with the job for the worker. But should employer based on this argumentation hire rather older workers than younger ones? There is much to be said against it. Young individuals are rather formable than older ones. Their ability to get new skills, especially special knowings of procedures of the firm, can rather be learned by young people. Furthermore, firms can pay fewer wages for young workers than for older ones. This is the case because older workers have more abilities and hence demand for higher wages.

But beside of the age of an employee, there are other important aspects. A further matching factor can be the gender of the employee. The question if a potential new worker is a man or a woman can be an important one - as well for the hiring process as for job satisfaction and quitting rates.

Many studies show differences between the job behaviour of men and women and the rates of quitting and unemployment. For instance, job satisfaction of men on the one hand and women on the other hand is the centrally theme of the paper of Hodson (Hodson 1989). He asked for differences in behaviour in the context of job characteristics, family characteristics and personal expectations. Main results of his research are differences in

- the focus in a certain work at a given level of job satisfaction
- condition of job satisfaction relative to the extent of the family responsibility
- individual expectations in evaluating the certain job.

In result, jobs are for women rather not the source of satisfaction but it seems that the family are. Men have a higher incentive to work hard and become therefore recognition in form of money, success in job, promotion, etc. Some empirical evidences show that the satisfaction of these points for men are lower (see 5.3). The level of satisfaction decline significantly if these acknowledgements come to nothing. If this is the case for working women, they benefit from their satisfaction with family.

These results have positive and negative features. With a family in the background and thus a source of satisfaction, women are more resistant in cases of job crisis. They do not life for work. Men can drift in a circle of dissatisfaction. No job might lead to a decline in satisfaction and this leads to less motivation to work. Hodson argues for example, that children have a significant positive impact on the satisfaction level of woman - but not on men (Hodson 1989).

But there are also some negative results of the differences in satisfaction sources. With another pool of satisfaction, women could be less motivated in their job, because the incentive to be successful is not as high as it is for men. Men try to work as hard as they can to be successful and hence satisfied. This counts also for woman - until they are no more successful. With being not successful, the rate of satisfaction sinks, which leads for women to an escape route in form of satisfaction by family. This leads to another important aspect. The quitting rate of women is significant higher than the one of men. The reason is again the difference in satisfaction source. For women, it might be easier to quit the job and care for the family. Partly, this could be a vestige of earlier times where woman are mostly the secondary wage earners. Such factors can lead to a significant handicap of women in the hiring process (see also 5.2).

The above-mentioned factors have also to be discussed in the organizational view. Firms invest in their workers - for instance with advanced training. Hence, the certain firm has costs now, which hopefully will be paying out in future. With a higher quitting rate of women, a payment default has a higher probability. This could lead to a favour for male workers and so a discrimination of women.

Another important point in the labor market matching difficulty might be how organizations, namely firms, can attract potential employees. This case affects as well the pecuniary part as the non-pecuniary. To become the best workers, firms do not only have to offer a high amount of money. Even if the pecuniary aspects are very well, potential employees could reject the offer. The higher the skills and education of the individual, the more important is the non-pecuniary aspect of a certain job. Reason for this is that persons who are educated very well and have many and high skilled abilities can in most cases choose between several jobs. Hence, a firm have first to raise the pecuniary aspect in terms of the amount of money. But with diminishing marginal utility of money (in higher levels of wages), this becomes less and less importance. Factors like satisfaction with the certain job, collegiality and so on are instead the reason why a person joins one firm and rejects the offer of the others.

In the economy of a certain state, individuals can not know the concrete determinants of a firm and otherwise. Hence, both parties have to show what they can and how they could help the other part. Based on the terms of asymmetrical information, one can see the organizational as well as the workers party as one with incomplete information about the other side. Therefore, both parts have to show their advantages to attract the other one and hence to achieve a match between them. On the organizational side this can be reached by signalling and screening of potential new employees. Thereby, signalling is a way to attract potential workers through the public image of a firm. Examples therefore can be advertising in TV and magazines or carrier days. Screening on the other side rather is a way to found employees instead of to be found by them. This term includes the whole hiring process and its determinants like searching for abilities, following employee referrals, etc.

In this context, different papers observed the signalling of firms through recruitment and image. Following the study of Fernandez, Castilla and Moore, there can be three explanations who measure the economic returns from hiring (Fernandez, Castilla et al. 2000). These three explanations, namely "richer pool", "better match" and "social enrichment" are competing in some points. Especially better match as a more pecuniary method and social enrichment as a more non-pecuniary can be seen as contrasts. The argumentation of the richer pool explanation is a trivial one. More and better applicants increase the hiring pool of the certain firm which result in an increase in economic turnover if new applicants get hired. If the certain referrer does not want to harm his or her firm with the employee referral or if he or she does not overestimate the estimation about the candidate or him- or herself, referral suggestions of employees are at least as good as usual applicants of the firm, if not even better. This is supported by the argument of reputation protection (see 4.1.1, mechanism c).

Better match theories are far more pecuniary aligned, for example with rewards for good employee referrals. This might be a good way to increase the incentive of a certain worker to suggest applicants. In any case, this way increases the pool of applicants. But pecuniary incentives might also bring along some problems. Provision incentives can mostly lead to too many acquisitions - here to too many suggestions of possible applicants. The value of the certain applicant suggestion will sink with high probability with the increase of the certain reward for an employee referral. Hence, pecuniary compensation for employee referrals can lead to a higher amount of potential applicants but the value of a certain candidate might decreases with higher rewards.

Social enrichment as a contrary to better match concentrates mainly on the social interaction of individuals after the hiring of the organization. So, this theory is rather an "after-hiring" one instead a "during-hiring" one, like the better match or richer pool explanations. Within this explanation, already in the firm working individuals and new ones get in a mentoring like situation. The mentor learns the mentee in on the job training the important parts of his or her job - at least in the theory. In reality, such social situations can lead to positive as well as negative effects for employer and employee. All in all, the employer has to notice that he can not rely too much on the employee referrals of the workers. Especially if the referrers try to include their friends into their organization, this might lead to some kind of problems. The above-mentioned example of the nurses who cover for one another has shown that hiring friends of workers is not at all a good idea. The right amount of social interaction has to predict by the employer regarding a hiring supported by an employee referral. Too much sociality between the workers can lead to an effect like the nurse example. However, too less social interaction after a hiring, considering the above-mentioned example of Bailey and Waldinger, is also bad for the organization - especially if the firm hires the applicant with regards to gain from the social enrichment factors. Predicting the right amount of expected social interaction is of crucial importance for the organization to stay at the same or even improve the productivity level.

However, better social relations between workers of a certain firm could increase the productivity. Considering the tendency of individuals to refer others like themselves (see 4.1.1, mechanism b), new hired workers can increase a homogenous procedure within the organization. Individuals work and think similar which lead to a straight way in the production. Considering this fact, there might also be some negative points. With many similar thinking persons, "thinking outside the box" effects decline significantly. Result of this could be that changes in the production, which needs other ways of thinking or doing, lead to serious problems for the workers. Diversity of workers might here be the better way. Thinkable are in this context that more complex organizations or productions, respectively, should keep some distance from the employers referrer mechanism. At least, before hiring a certain applicant through such a referral, the firm should expend more effort in the hiring process. However, diversity of workers should not be necessary for easy production procedures or organizations with linier methods.

Within the diversity context one can implement the explanation of better match. Rewards for employee referrals might exist or increase with the size of a firm. Following this thinking, one might distinguish four kinds of organizations. There are small and large sized firms with linier or diverse production procedures. Following the above-mentioned argumentation and logically thinking, the diversity of production decreases when the size of a firm increases. Background of this can be the following. The smaller a firm is, the more has the certain worker to do within the production process. In addition, in this case a worker could also do some stuff in other parts of the firm, for example as a temporary help in case of illness of another worker. If the size of the certain firm increases, the amount of workers increases, too. The certain individual now has to do more and more the same parts of the production procedure. Furthermore, things like temporary help situations happen rarer.

A crucial point of labor market matching is the one of mismatching. Over- and undereducation can lead to hard distortions and reduce the productivity of a certain firm and hence the welfare of a state. Although undereducated individuals try to do their best in an "above" job and so raise their own productivity ceiling near to their ability margin, the overall productivity might decrease without a perfect allocation of skills of persons and jobs.

The danger of the factor of skill-job mismatching is discussed above especially in several articles. Considering the financial crisis and the consequences, the over- und under-skilled employee can harm as well the employee itself as the employer. Especially in the article of Faberman and Mazumder, a critical development for the middle skilled workers is happening after the financial crisis in the US labor market. Although the low skilled individuals become in the post-crisis years an only marginal higher unemployment rate than before and the high skilled workers stays at the same level, the increase in unemployment of the middle skilled persons is significantly high.

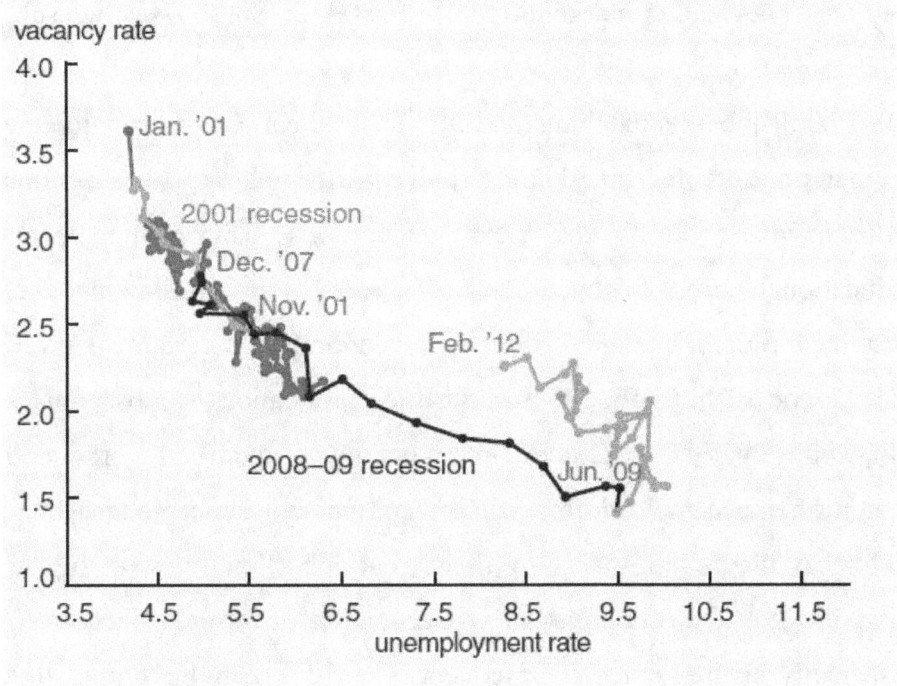

As a result of this different unemployment rates, the employees search for other jobs - maybe in sectors which requires other, namely higher or lower, skills than the certain person has. This leads to mismatching and hence to a loss in productivity.

As a further example of the dangerous consequences of skill mismatching for the certain worker, an article of the Telegraph has shown a report of the ILO (Peacock 2013). Thereby, the job situation of UK workers in context of the financial crisis and the following skill mismatch are displayed. Following the ILO, such a process, "hampers the allocation of labor and will put upward pressure on employment rates". The global unemployment rises in 2012 with one quarter in the advanced economies and with three quarters in other regions. This lead to market effects in East Asia, South Asia and Sub-Saharan Africa.

With skill-job mismatching and all its implications, especially the higher pressure for unemployed individuals, this can have serious consequences. First, the next generations can change their educational aims to become later "safe" jobs. Following this argumentation, a change of the whole economy of a certain state can be the end of this process. Second, the reallocation of jobs reduces the welfare of a state, as above-mentioned. Overqualified workers do not further use their skills until the ceiling and hence reduce their effort to the requirements of the actual job. Finally, with higher pressure for the unemployed persons, diseases might increase - especially mental ones. Consequences of this can be things like "lower quality" workforces for the economy, higher rates of missing if the unemployed persons who are in jobs or higher costs for health insurances.

In addition, educational as well as skill mismatching occurs from different failures of employers and employees. One main failure is the non-transparency of vacancies. Employees do not exactly know the required skills for the certain job. Employees do not know what skills an applicant have because the focus on applicants is rather on the term of qualifications than on the one of skills. Qualifications thereby, summarizes what a certain person had complete respectively what this person had achieved so far. In contrast, skills rather mean the characteristics or abilities of an individual, for instance a good oral presentation skill or good technical abilities. A more general example could be the following: A certain qualification is educated as a motor mechanic whereas the skill might be that this person has good technical abilities. Thus, qualifications do not mean that the potential worker is capable to do his or her new job well. Skills are rather a function to measure.

All in all, skill mismatching is a crucial factor of badly labor market matching. Beside the above-mentioned point, there are other things that can lead to mismatching. Over time, the sectors of a certain market change. Jobs, which have a high demand today, can be obsolete tomorrow. Considering this, the skills and abilities of a certain individual are one time very special and result in good job offers and high wages and at another point of time, these skills are common or no more useful within a firm. An interesting example of this thinking is the above-mentioned one of polarization where the introduction of computers reduces the jobs in middle skilled sectors (see 3.5). As above-mentioned, a certain market has to be different skill groups of workers. Thereby, normally a low-skilled, middle-skilled and high-skilled group exist (Faberman and Mazumder 2012). Every kind of skill is needed to ensure a sustainable economy. With an increase in development of a certain country, the amount of middle- and high-skilled workers might increase, too. There are more analytical and non-routine jobs within the economy. The more a certain country is a developing one, the higher might the rate of low-skilled jobs because the branches of work are also rather low-skilled ones. Examples therefore can be the field of agriculture. Following Rohrbach-Schmidt and Tiemann, the prevalence of the personal computer leads to a declining middle-skilled job variety. Reason for this so called "computerization" is that the personal computer occupied the middle-skilled jobs. Considering the fact that a wide availability of computers is rather the fact in the industrialized countries, this might be a problem of developed and not developing countries. Hence, one can conclude that with the rising of a developing to a developed country, first the high-skilled jobs increase and then the middle-skilled ones decrease.

So far, one can see that non-pecuniary aspects play a role for a certain individual. But furthermore, non-pecuniary aspects between several individuals are important. The above discussed example of employee referrals has clarified this. In the section of weak and strong ties, one can also see how important relations to individuals who are already working in the organization are. Employee referrals based on this term in some ways because such referrals are based mostly on friendships between individuals. The tie approach does not try to explain the side of the already working person but the one of the applicant. If the certain firm wants to hire a new worker, the applicants who have friends respectively relationships within the firm have also mostly advantages as opposed to the one who have no friends or relationships. The using of ties between currently workers and potential new workers is defined by the costs of a hiring. Hire new persons is always costly - for both sides of the hiring process.

The applicant has to show his or her competences through references, qualifications and so on via signalling. The costs of this can be monetary ones, for instance fees for curses or costs for copies of honours. But costs can also be the spent time for get the competences. Nevertheless, all of these are opportunity costs for the applicant because he or she could in the same time also work for another firm or do something else instead of applying for the certain organization.

For a certain hiring firm, costs are also either monetary or time consuming, one or both, for similar reasons. But as opposite to the applicant, the firm can save costs through social ties between worker and applicant. On the one hand, the formal sight can be seen through the competences of an applicant and gives the firm a frame of his abilities (but as above-mentioned no full view because of skills). But on the other hand, the informal sight of this applicant through a worker of the firm can save much time and money for screening and furthermore help the applicant to get the job if the worker gives the hiring personal an employee referral. The formal screening mechanisms might not be necessary.

Getting information through firm members becomes the more importance the higher skilled the position to hire is. This might be the case because the higher a position is the higher are the necessary skills the applicant has to bring along. This could be a reason for the job of headhunters. Headhunters find high qualified, high skilled persons and relate them to a firm who have instructs them. As a certain point of screening costs, it might be cheaper to employ a headhunter than to hire the false individual and bear the risks of failures of him or her. In addition, with the hiring of a headhunter, the costs of screening disappear. Instead, a company has to pay the headhunter for finding an appropriate applicant.

Best Matching Preconditions of Employees

So far, there is a wide range of studies of different matching factors within the labor market. The importance of terms like job satisfaction is, considering the results of dissatisfaction, unassailable. Organizations want to hire workers who grow with the firm (expect these workers are easy to substitute, for example low paid persons with no skills where a dismissal has no costs in form of loss of production or skill). In general, firms try to become individuals who see the employer as a chance to make career. Every sector needs some kind of hard skills. Branches with contact to customers and relationships within colleagues need soft skills like friendliness, for instance. Firms send employees to advanced training to become better workers and so a higher and more efficient production. Every side can gain from these deals. But some sorts of employee are more likely to be "non-cooperative" about these "agreement".

Given the study of Quinn and Staines, there is a U-shaped form of job satisfaction with age (Clark, Oswald et al. 1996). Hence, potential workers are motivated at the beginning of their career. Then, with the age of about 30, the motivation sinks. After this bottom, workers are with every year a bit more motivated until they stop working for pension. This means for firms: workers in the early thirties are at least motivated to do some job. This consideration has a positive and a negative view. On the one hand, hiring and investing in such individuals promise with a lower probability better skilled employees. These persons are not as motivated as, for instance, the starting or older workers. This may result in a higher degree of failed advanced trainings and hence in wasted time and money for the firm.

But this is only the short-range view. On the other hand, workers in the early thirties increase from now with every year their motivation until the pension. In comparison to older workers, this group has far more years of potential skill gaining and therefore is a more valuable ground for investment. Another positive aspect of hiring this group is the above-mentioned OJS, the "on-the-job search" of persons. Given the low motivation, workers in the early thirties have a lower job satisfaction and so a higher chance for on-the-job search. This probability increases further with the experience or respectively the skills of the certain worker (higher educated workers are earlier dissatisfied with a job and hence search earlier for better employees). Thus, the chance of getting an individual of this group, and so a chance of a valuable long-range investment is quite large.

The advantages and disadvantages of the other two subgroups result from the above-mentioned assumptions. Advantage of the young, starting workers group is the long potential gain from investing in these people. Disadvantage is the inexperience and the following bottom in motivation. Furthermore, some studies observe a motivation of young individuals, which is not as high as in the U-shaped variant (Quinn and Staines 1979). Hence, the motivation level might increase not until the mid-thirties, which decline the chance to gaining skills with advanced training until this point in life of this group.

The older group has the advantage of a high degree of job satisfaction (amongst other reasons through a more realistic view of career making(Clark, Oswald et al. 1996)). Furthermore, older workers are in average more skilled than younger ones. But hire, integrate and invest in older workers is in long-range and so on consideration of a soon retire not as valuable as in younger people.

There are two more theories about job satisfaction and age (see 4.2.1). The second by Hulin and Smith is likewise the U-shaped function (Hulin and Smith 1965): Individuals are more motivated with every year of working. Hence, the motivation in the beginning is very low. Comparing to the U-shaped function, this is like a change of motivation between the early thirty old workers and the young workers of the theory of Hulin and Smith. For firms, this changes the priority of hiring. The older a person, the more motivated and the more satisfied he or she is. However, an investment in this person is more risky with every year of life because the worker is closer to the retirement.

The last theory is a quite different one: Like the second theory, a consistent increase of motivation is notified for workers with every year. But in this theory, a terminal period is reached in one point of time. The consequence of the beginning of this period is a significant decline in motivation. This means: young individuals are not motivated at all, start to work, gets more motivated with every year of work, then reach the terminal period and loss a high degree of motivation. For organizations, this is a case, reverse to the U-shaped function. Consequence of this is that the workers in the middle of age are the best ones to hire. There are some years until the retirement as well as there are already some skills of the potential employees. The young section is not motivated, but has a lot of years until the knock out from the labor marked due to retirement. The worst situation is the one of the old workers. They are not motivated and firms rather invest in persons with a bigger future relevant to work. In this theory, the only advantage might be the high skills of old workers. Hence, it is difficult to decide on the base of age if a certain applicant is motivated. Several theories show several results. Thus, this determinant seems not to be a good one to hire workers.

Another important aspect of hiring someone can be the gender of a person. In organizational view, investing in men could be more valuable than in women. Studies show that women have a higher chance of quit the job in favour of being unemployed respectively be a housewife and mother. The incentive for men to be successful in a certain job is higher. Men identify themselves with their success in job (see 4.2.1). Hence, job satisfaction is linked to job success for men. Quitting has therefore a quite lower chance in case of men. Satisfaction through the family relieves the compulsion to be successful in job for women. This leads to a higher quitting rate.

In organizational view, this arguments lead to a systematic disadvantage for women. Firms want to invest in their human capital, namely their workers. The chance of getting a gain from these investments is for women lower, given the above-mentioned assumptions. In the real context, this view led to dubious questions towards women about the planning of pregnancy and children. Nowadays, women get exhorted to not answer these questions in case of discrimination. Hence, job descriptions contain mostly a passage, where, in equally qualifications, woman are "favoured hired". However, considering the fact that a normally potential employee can not take a look into the hiring procedure, employers do not have to decide about a hiring on base of this passage. Thus, to be a woman can be a crucial disadvantage in the hiring process.

Similar to the higher quitting rate of women regarding to their satisfaction from their family is a higher education for the quitting term. Individuals who have a better educational level might rather be dissatisfied with their current job. The study of Clark and Oswald show that higher educated workers tend to urge as well pecuniary as non-pecuniary resources (Clark and Oswald 1996). Hence, for a given job with a given pecuniary and non-pecuniary level, the rate of job satisfaction increases the more, the less the education of a certain individuals is.

This implies a difficult problem for a certain firm. Firms want to hire the best individuals because this lead to the best (production) results. However, with hiring a good skilled person, the firm have to invest more money and non-pecuniary advantages in the contract to be sure that the level of dissatisfaction not increase. The contract has to be good enough to justify the value of the high potential worker on the one hand. But on the other hand, if the contract is too good, the investment in the certain individual is too high - and so not worthwhile for the firm.

Thus, the hiring of high skilled respectively high educated workers is not easy for firms. Firms should only invest in such type of individuals if the costs of a good contract respectively the investment in the future result in a payoff and a gain for the firm. In this case, both sides are satisfied: The worker has a good job satisfaction because his work is appreciated. The firm has well-educated employees and thus a good chance to persist in the market.

All the above-mentioned circumstances for individuals neglect that there are some individuals who are neither searching for a job nor have one. Regarding the theory of search, this can not happen. Van Ophem already addresses the point of unemployed individuals. Following search theory, unemployment only leads to one procedure - search for a job. In real world circumstances there can be many other factors which influence the decisions of an individual and in the current context if the unemployed individual search for a new job or not. These factors do not exist in the theory of search except the person searches already for a job. In this case, pecuniary and non-pecuniary factors come into mind and influence the decision of an individual. One can see this process like a decision tree. The first decision of an unemployed person is normally if search for a work or not. But in the context of search theory, this decision does not exist.

So, in real world context, there is at this point a decision - in the theory of search not.

If one assumes that the person follows the search theory and wants a new job, the next decision comes into mind - takes a certain job (offer) or rejects them. This leads to another possible weakness of the search theory model. Following the assumptions of the theory of search, individuals who search become a certain amount of possible new job offers. In difference to this theory, the real world searching process for a job can lead to no new job possibilities. Further factors that diminish or increase the chance of job offers are not taken into account like the branch of the worker, his abilities or the stage of the economy in the business cycle (namely recession or expansion).

Finally, if there are an amount of job offers, the individual decide to choose the one with the highest reservation utility - the utility the individual wants to have after compare costs of search with the gain from the new job. Thereby, the terms of costs are as well as the ones of utility relatively clear formulated. But in difference to the real world context, a person take in the theory of search the job offer, who has the best reservation utility. In the real world, this has not to be the necessary case. Although, non-pecuniary aspects of job decision can formulated as wide as one wants, an individual can choose finally a job, which is not the best for him for several reasons. An example can be an abruptly illness of the certain individual and thereby a waiver for the job with the best reservation utility because this would jeopardizes the person's health too much. But this example might also lead to a new search round and hence to a decision tree without the job offer. Furthermore, the illness and hence the health risk can be added to the costs of an acceptation of the job and so reduces the reservation utility. This can lead to a new decision because now the job is not further the best choice.

As a last determinant of the "ideal" worker suggestion, racial harassment plays a crucial role in the hiring process of firms and their potential new workers. Linked to the "optimal worker" thesis one tries to give above, this is not only the case for women versus men and the relations to job satisfaction and possible quitting rates. An at least equally important form of discrimination is racial harassment in. The above-mentioned study of Bertrand and Mullainathan of a different amount of callbacks for White and African-American sounding names underlines the importance of this problem. The fact of a more different way to become a job for "not White sounding names" suggests that there might be a kind of price for the name of an individual. This price can be seen in monetary sense, for instance in form of the lost job possibility. Furthermore, it might have a social price.

Not at least, a more difficult job search for disadvantaged social groups might lead to a higher unemployment because of the difficulty as well as a possible frustration of the individuals. This higher unemployment of a certain group underlines the doubts of employers in this group. Finally, with an underlined doubt, the degree of racial harassment increases.

All in all, one has to cherish that the hiring process for firms is not a trivial procedure. Many factors have to be taken into account to find the best new employee. One the one hand, employees have to improve their abilities and do lifelong learning to attract employers and get many and good job offers. On the other hand, the employer has the duty to avoid discrimination of women, persons of a certain age and ethnic minorities. This is not only a morale decree. With neglect such groups of applicants, organizations prevent to hire possible good employees because they separate them out or handle them disadvantageous.

5.2   Empirical evidence of pecuniary and non-pecuniary aspects in the labor market

In Cornelißen's paper, the factor of job satisfaction as well as the search for and the change of jobs are supported by empirical evidence from Germany (Cornelißen 2009). The data of the paper includes West German workers from the age of 16 until 60 and is used from a household survey of the German Socio-Economic panel (GSOEP) from 1984 to 2003. The total number of participants was 11,294. Beside the question of how much a certain worker is satisfied with his or her job (with a range from 0 to 10; 0 for "totally unhappy", 10 for "totally happy")), there are also several questions about different job characteristics like wages, work time or worries about job security (surveyed for each years) and some like task diversity or relations with colleagues (surveyed in recent years). In his study, Cornelißen concludes that West German workers are on average satisfied with their jobs. This can be shown through some results like the points for job satisfaction.

Variable	Unit of measurement	Female Mean	Male Mean	Total Mean	Std. Dev.	Min	Max
Job satisfaction	(d)	7.29	7.33	7.31	1.94	0	10
Activity corresponds to job	(a)	0.65	0.63	0.63	0.48	0	1
Fringe benefits	(a)	0.92	0.95	0.94	0.24	0	1
Some worries about job security	(a)	0.05	0.04	0.04	0.20	0	1
Strong worries about job security	(a)	0.29	0.33	0.31	0.46	0	1
Fixed-term contract	(a)	0.06	0.08	0.07	0.26	0	1
Conflicts, difficulties with supervisor	(a)	0.02	0.03	0.03	0.16	0	1
Exposed to adverse environment	(a)	0.07	0.22	0.17	0.37	0	1
Get along well with colleagues	(a)	0.80	0.79	0.80	0.40	0	1
Hard manual labor	(a)	0.09	0.14	0.12	0.32	0	1
Stress	(a)	0.27	0.31	0.30	0.46	0	1
Independence	(a)	0.39	0.40	0.40	0.49	0	1
Influence on pay and promotion of others	(c)	0.13	0.26	0.21	0.41	0	1
Learning opportunities	(a)	0.32	0.38	0.36	0.48	0	1
Shift work	(c)	0.14	0.20	0.18	0.38	0	1
Strict control of performance	(c)	0.45	0.52	0.50	0.50	0	1
Task diversity	(a)	0.58	0.67	0.64	0.48	0	1
Subjective probability of promotion	(b)	0.12	0.21	0.18	0.38	0	1
Deviation of actual from desired work time	Weekly hours	6.35	6.24	6.28	7.63	0	70
Actual work time	Weekly hours	34.66	43.36	40.14	9.90	1.00	80.00
Logarithm of net wage	Log monthly wage	6.75	7.31	7.11	0.52	5.00	9.07
Wage growth rate	Diff. log wage	0.07	0.05	0.06	0.21	−2.15	2.40

$N = 11,294$

(a) Fraction saying the job characteristic applies to their job
(b) Coded from 1 = unlikely to 4 = certain
(c) Fraction saying the job characteristic applies or partly applies to their job
(d) Coded in integers from 0 = totally unhappy to 10 = totally happy

In mean, women and men are relatively satisfied with their current jobs. Men reach a score of 7.33 of 10 and women 7.29. Most of the other questions of the survey, rated from zero to ten, show that there are no significantly differences between of women and men. The level of stress is similar for women (0.27) and men (0.31) as well as collegiality (women 0.80, men 0.79) or independence (women 0.39, men 0.40). An interesting difference exists in the factor of task diversity. Following the survey, the interviewed women have significantly lower task diversity (0.58 of 1) than the interviewed men (0.67). Hence, the tasks women have to do in their jobs in West Germany in the time from 1984 to 2003 were more monotonous than the one of men. Following this argument and the result of the Logarithm of the net wages of both (women 6.75, men 7.31), one can conclude that women has in this time in West Germany rather low skilled jobs. With higher task diversity, the wage rate should rise, too.

Another interesting result of the survey is the work time and the deviation of this time from the wishes of time for work of the certain person. In average, men work around 43.36 hours per week. In contrast, women work about 34.66 hours per week, which is about nine hours or 20 per cent less than men. But both, men and women, desire to work in average 6.28 hours less per week (women 6.35, men 6.24). This result can be explained through the approach of satisfaction of the family. Men define them through their work and get satisfaction from job successes. However, women become satisfaction rather through their family and their children. This might explain why women have the desire to work less, although they already work 20 per cent less than men do.

Satisfaction with the certain job is an important factor of matching. Low job satisfaction leads to more quits and so a higher fluctuation. Most of the quitting individuals will find jobs because quitting the current job based on dissatisfaction include on-the-job search. However, a certain part of the quitting persons will not find another job respectively do not want to find one. This can lead to an increase of the rate of unemployment. A study of Clark shows that job satisfaction levels of women and men in comparison and how satisfied each group in sub themes comparing to job satisfaction (Clark 1997). Therefore, Clark use data "from wave 1 of the British Household Panel Survey (BHPS)" (Clark 1997, S. 347). Nearly 10,000 adult persons were interviewed in 5500 households from September to December 1991. There is a scale from 1 to 7(1 for "not satisfied at all", 7 for "completely satisfied") for the overall job satisfaction question as well as for sub themes like wage rate, job security or promotion prospects in relation to the term job satisfaction. Amongst others, this study shows that woman have in all sub groups a higher satisfaction with the current job than men have.

Type of job satisfaction	Women	Men	All	t-statistic on gender difference
Mean reported job satisfaction levels				
Overall	5.71	5.31	5.50	9.56
Promotion prospects	4.36	4.22	4.28	2.38
Total pay	4.65	4.33	4.48	5.87
Relations at work	5.86	5.47	5.66	8.36
Job security	5.41	5.01	5.20	7.39
Initiative	5.87	5.80	5.84	1.59
Actual work itself	5.78	5.56	5.67	5.08
Hours	5.56	5.08	5.31	9.79
Percentage highly satisfied				
Overall	65.0	52.9	58.7	8.88
Promotion prospects	32.7	29.6	31.0	2.23
Total pay	38.7	31.2	34.8	5.70
Relations at work	69.5	60.8	65.0	6.48
Job security	59.1	50.2	54.5	6.40
Initiative	70.5	68.6	69.5	1.53
Actual work itself	66.7	60.6	63.6	4.55
Hours	60.4	47.9	53.9	9.06

Note: The number of observations varies slightly with the satisfaction measure used. There are 2501 and 2693 observations on female and male workers respectively for overall job satisfaction. All numbers refer to weighted data.

The highest differences between women and men are in the fields of work hours (women 5.56, men 5.08), job security (women 5.41, men 5.01) and relations to work (women 5.86, men 5.47). The overall job satisfaction draws the same picture with a satisfaction level of 5.71 of 7 for women in comparison of 5.31 of 7 for men. Furthermore, Clark illustrates the highly satisfied percentages (from zero to 100) of women and men for the overall satisfaction and the sub themes. Here, 65 per cent of women are highly satisfied with their work versus only 52.9 per cent of the men. The highest levels of satisfaction for women are the fields of initiative (70.5), relations to work (69.5) and actual work itself (66.7). The highest differences between women and men are in the area of work hours (women 60.4, men 47.9), relations to work (women 69.5, men 60.8) and job security (women 59.1, men 50.2). Both parties are relatively dissatisfied with the terms of promotion prospects (women 32.7, men 29.6) and total pay (women 38.7, men 31.2).

These results support the approach of different sources of satisfaction for men and woman again. Although women get a lower average wage rate, the satisfaction with this amount is higher than the one of better paid men. Comparing the above-mentioned study of Cornelißen and this one, women are in average worse paid but also more satisfied with their work. This might come from the satisfaction factor of the family which relates the needed satisfaction from job. However, the needed satisfaction of men rather has to come from their job because a given family or children does not matter as much as for women. Thus, men have to get satisfaction through job successes and hence they are more dissatisfied with their work hours, promotion prospects and total pay - compared to women as well as in general.

Clark and Oswald have analysed the satisfaction of 5195 British employees with their current job. Therefore, the workers give point for their satisfaction from 1 ("not satisfied at all") to 7 (completely satisfied").

The results of this sample are as follows: Most of the respondents give their job satisfaction the full score of 7 - namely more than 31 percent. 6 out of 7 points is the next highest rate with about 26 percent. Further results are: 5 of 7 with 19.1 percent, 4 of 7 with 12.6

percent, 3 of 7 with 4.6 percent, 2 of 7 with 1.7 percent and finally 1 of 7 with 3.4 percent (Clark and Oswald 1996).

So, all in all, more than the half of the respondents gives their job satisfaction a score of 6 respectively 7 out of 7. Less than 10 percent of the respondents are unsatisfied with their job (3, 2 or 1 out of 7). Hence, in this sample, workers seem happy with their current job situation.

A question who has to be asked is the one about racism in job searching. An appearance of this fact can influence the matching of employee and employer eminently. The opinions about racism in job searching as well as during the job are wide. Bertrand and Mullainathan found in a study in Boston and Chicago a significant difference between callbacks on applications between very White and very African-American sounding names (Bertrand and Mullainathan 2003). The certain jobs were from ads for help-wanted in Boston and Chicago newspapers.

Thereby, they observed a 50 percent higher callback rate for White sounding names. Namely, the fictional White sounding names have to send about ten resumes to become one callback. African-American sounding names have to send about 15 applications to become a callback.

The existing of racial harassment in the labor market has resulted in some studies about this theme and to some empirical evidences, too. The paper of Shields and Price observes the factor of racial harassment within the labor market of nurses in England. Therefore, a "survey of NHS nursing staff undertaken by the Policy Studies

Institute and commissioned by the Department of Health" was used (Beishon, Virdee et al. 1995, Shields and Price 2002, S. 297). The generated sample of this survey is about 14,000 nurses, which reflects a response rate of 62 per cent. Shields and Price observed those 1203 nurses who reported that they have another ethnicity than white.

The table below shows the results of racial harassment while working.

	Racial harassment from staff			Racial harassment from patients			Sample size
	Frequent	Infrequent	Never	Frequent	Infrequent	Never	
Black African	8.3	40.1	51.5	14.5	54.9	30.6	324
	(1.5)	(2.7)	(2.8)	(2.0)	(2.8)	(2.6)	
Black Caribbean	5.6	29.7	64.6	9.1	58.8	32.1	461
	(1.1)	(2.1)	(2.2)	(1.3)	(2.3)	(2.2)	
South Asian	8.4	30.5	61.1	5.8	50.5	43.7	190
	(2.0)	(3.4)	(3.6)	(1.7)	(3.6)	(3.6)	
South-east Asian	4.0	28.1	68.0	7.5	48.7	43.9	228
	(1.3)	(3.0)	(3.1)	(1.7)	(3.3)	(3.3)	
All non-whites	6.5	32.3	61.2	9.7	54.5	35.7	1203
	(0.7)	(1.4)	(1.4)	(0.9)	(1.4)	(1.4)	
	(2265)	**(11,255)**	**(21,325)**	**(3380)**	**(18,991)**	**(12,440)**	**(34,845)**

Note: Standard errors in parentheses; authors' calculations of the number of NHS nurses (1994) in bold.

The comparison of all non-white nurses of the survey shows that two of five nurses were susceptible to racial harassment from staff (frequent 6.5, infrequent 32.3). The results of racial harassment by patients are even higher. 54.5 per cent of the nurses were frequently or infrequently susceptible to a form of racial harassment. Thereby, Black African and Back Caribbean nurses get higher scores of harassment than South-east Asian nurses.

The results of this study as well as the results of other ones could have a huge influence on the choice of ethnic group on their future jobs. Considering the facts above-mentioned, young men and women can choose to do another job apprenticeship. This might lead to a bottleneck in some branches, for instance in the nursing sector. To avoid such bottlenecks, racial harassment reduction in jobs with a high ethnic minority part might be a key factor.

It seems that mismatching is a crucial factor in the labor market. Within these term, educational and skill mismatching have to be distinguished. There are several studies who observe if mismatching influence the labor market and how it does. One of these studies is from Hersch (Hersch 1991). She asked in the context of overeducation, and hence, educational mismatching, 414 male and 213 female employees of manufacturing and warehouse firms in the Eugene, Oregon area in 1986. Each of the eighteen participating firms has over 40 employees. Within the study, Hersch distinguished between man and woman, white and not white and married and not married. Primarily, she asked the persons about their job satisfaction, quit intention, wage rate and, as the main point of the study, about the years of required education and the currently education.

Variable	Mean	Variance
educational level	4.10	0.68
educational level unknown	0.05	0.05
age	36.11	115.44
age2	1419.70	697776.21
tenure	8.78	68.43
civil servant	0.40	0.24
female	0.35	0.23
course	0.17	0.14
too high educational level	0.33	0.22
too low educational level	0.08	0.07
good promotion chances	0.34	0.22
unemployment expectation	0.11	0.10
unpaid overtime	1.33	12.68
commute	19.42	311.49

Findings has been given in ranges from zero to one (like married, white, quit intention), hence, yes or no questions respectively questions with a range from zero to 100 percent and furthermore as an amount (like wage rate, years of education, experience). In addition, the level of satisfaction has been asked with a level from zero (not at all satisfied) to ten (very satisfied).

Although it is only one questionnaire, the results are very interesting. Some figures are quite logical. Men get a higher wage rate than women (9.99 versus 7.54), and a higher experience (14.59 versus 12.16). The former one can be partly explained by the latter one.

Furthermore women could have less work experience because of above-mentioned results like the other sources of satisfaction. This is supported by the questionnaire. The job satisfaction of men is lower than the one of women (6.35 versus 6.74). But another above-mentioned point is not supported here: In this case, the quit intention of men are higher than the one of women (0.46 versus 0.38). This result could be explained with the closer job relationship of men. The quitting rate increases if an individual is not satisfied with a certain job. This factor is stronger for men than for women.

Another interesting fact is the rate of marriage. In an above part, one argues that mostly women are the co-workers of men respectively they work for some years until a certain age before they devote their role as a mother. This can be supported by this study. While men are in 72 percent in a marriage (0.72), women are only in 57 percent (0.57). However, one has to regard the year of publishing of the study (1991). Nowadays, the marriage percentage might be look much different.

Van Ophem performs some empirical evidence in his paper to underline the importance of future wages and non-wage characteristics as well as present wages and non-wage characteristics. Therefore, he uses from an OSA Labor Market Survey from April 1985. Within this survey, 4020 individuals with an age between 16 and 60 were asked about their present labor market position. Furthermore, the persons have to estimate their change in labor market position from January 1, 1980 up to April 1985. In addition, personal characteristics and educational backgrounds were asked.

The results of the survey are various (see table 3).

Variable	Definition	Males	Females
WAGE	= hourly wage.	9.99 (4.05)	7.54 (2.81)
SATISFACTION	= ranking of job satisfaction on a scale of 0 to 10 from not at all satisfied to very satisfied	6.35 (2.49)	6.74 (2.61)
QUIT INTENTION	= 1 if worker is somewhat or very likely to make a genuine effort to change employment in the next 12 months; 0 otherwise	0.46 (0.50)	0.38 (0.49)
OJT	= weeks of company provided on-the-job training	10.13 (31.19)	6.15 (19.36)
EDUCATION	= years of schooling completed	13.33 (2.07)	12.95 (1.58)
REQUIRED EDUCATION	= years of schooling needed to perform the job, not just to be hired	11.67 (2.60)	11.68 (2.71)
EXPERIENCE	= years of full-time work experience since age 18	14.59 (11.03)	12.16 (9.58)
TENURE	= years of tenure with present employer	7.33 (7.14)	5.42 (5.93)
HANDICAPPED	= 1 if physical condition limits work; 0 otherwise	0.07 (0.26)	0.08 (0.27)
WHITE	= 1 if worker is white; 0 otherwise	0.95 (0.21)	0.94 (0.23)
MARRIED	= 1 if married; 0 otherwise	0.72 (0.45)	0.57 (0.50)
UNION	= 1 if worker's job is covered by a union contract; 0 otherwise	0.33 (0.47)	0.35 (0.48)
Sample size		414	213

For instance, from the 2081 wage-earners who were retained search 271 in April 1985 for a job, 1810 do not. Further results are a mean tenure level of 8.78. 40 percent of the people of the sample are in a civil servant position. The really interesting results in this context are the ones about over- and undereducation. For this sample, 33 percent argues that they are overqualified, only eight percent things that they are underqualified. In addition the promotion chances were asked. 34 percent state that they have good chances to get a promotion soon.

On the other side, 11 percent thinks that they are unemployed in the near future (Van Ophem 1991).

5.3 Importance of pecuniary and non-pecuniary Aspects by Comparison

The sections of pecuniary and non-pecuniary aspects have given an impression of the problem of labor market matching between workers and firms as well as the part of discussion. Both parts are important for a functional matching. Organizations respectively firms try to hire the best individuals for their firms considering a more effective or higher production level with the new worker. They see in a new employee an investment - characterized by costs at the beginning, but with a long-range gain for the firm in terms of money, efficiency and, not at least, social. Workers as the other part of the matching plan are influenced by a wide range of pecuniary and non-pecuniary aspects. Money plays a significantly role in a certain job application. However, non-pecuniary aspects include without limitations job satisfaction, motivation or collegiality and is also of great importance for a long-range successful matching between employee and employer.

Within the non-pecuniary aspects, the factor of job satisfaction seems to play a crucial role. The decision of doing a certain job furthermore or not is dependent on this key factor. Thus, the higher the degree of dissatisfaction with the job, the higher is the on-the-job search (OJS), the rate of quitting increases and the motivation decreases. The worker is otherwise engaged or tends to make more mistakes. Consequently, the level of collegiality might sink. Hence, with a high level of job dissatisfaction, the productivity of the certain worker sinks as well as the productivity of the other workers.

Non-pecuniary literature has increasing over the last 20 years, compared to the time before. Many non-pecuniary aspects are in focus now, so for instance job satisfaction, rate of quitting or racial harassment as well in the job as in the hiring process. Many factors influence the different decisions of an individual to choose a certain job, to get hired by the organization, to be dissatisfied with the conquered job and to search for another one or quit the currently work. There are many studies who give a try about why women and men have as well different imaginations about an appropriate job as well as younger and older employees have. It is a fact that pecuniary aspects, first of all the amount of money in terms of wage rates, is not the key to have the best and most satisfied workers in the own firm. Matching between applicant and organization is influenced by much more - not at least seen in the section about employee referral.

Whereas neo-classical and pecuniary models rather try to understand the behaviour of employees and employer through wage rates, time division, effort and risk behaviour, other, non-pecuniary, approaches focus more on social relations, friendships or satisfaction. The explanations of Fernandez, Castilla and Moore (see 4.2.1) about richer pool, better match and social enrichment within the theory of hiring as a crucial part of the matching process underline the interaction of both parts. Solely one model, either pecuniary or non-pecuniary, can not exist. If for example only terms like wage rates and leisure time, effort and risk behaviour would count for employers, workers get dissatisfied and a high rate of quits reduce the productivity until the organization has to leave the market. On the other side, if only non-pecuniary aspects were important, no one would work. A crucial part of working incentive is to assure the subsistence. This goal can only be achieved if the person gets a compensation for his effort, namely an amount of money. Hence, pecuniary aspects maintain the main characteristics of working every day. Non-pecuniary aspects assure a livelong incentive to perform over the baseline of subsistence assurance and improve the one personality.

All in all, neo-classical model have to revised respectively they are out of time. The classical income-leisure model does not work well. Many other factors influence the decision of an individual. So, these factors do this in the context of labor market matching, too. Aspects can be of pecuniary or non-pecuniary nature. The former one plays rather a role in neo-classical models than the latter one. Pecuniary reasons in job models are given in the based model of income versus leisure.

6   Result

Why do individuals work? And if they decide to work, what are the incentives of choose a certain job and reject another? Finally, why hires a firm a certain applicant and why another not? There are several aspects, pecuniary as well as non-pecuniary ones, which try to answer this question. In fact, matching in the labor market is a difficult situation which is influenceable by a great amount of possible factors. One the one hand, employees has a clearly monetary sense in working for a certain firm. They want to reach better states in their lifestyle, want to fight against basic needs like hunger, thirst and homelessness. But on the other hand, if individuals have the opportunity between some jobs, non-pecuniary aspects come into focus. Aspects like job satisfaction, motivation or carrier and further become a higher importance. Hand in hand with the increase of the importance of non-pecuniary aspects, the significance of pecuniary aspects decreases. Given the assumption that most of the individuals have the possibility to work, the non-monetary conditions are even more important than the monetary ones. This might be not at least the case because the absence of non-pecuniary incentives in a certain job leads to higher quitting rates which in turn rises the rate of unemployment because not every worker who is dissatisfied with his or her job decide to do on-the-job search. Some, especially women, labourers quit their job and are afterwards unemployed. Again, these assumptions are mainly the case in a world with given possibilities to work. In addition, such procedures might be happening rather in economies with stable institutions and preferably in social welfare states. Here, the above-mentioned basic needs are furthermore satisfiable.

Pecuniary and non-pecuniary aspects hold for organizations, too. As one can see in the section about acceptance wages, there are pecuniary incentives which can lead to quits of good workers and to morale risks which result in a lower productivity of the certain firm. Hence, pecuniary things like wage rate or efficiency labourers are important - in the example of acceptance wages even for the worker and the firm. But there are also other instances of significant pecuniary parts of labor market matching. In most cases, the productivity of the organization is harmed if the pecuniary aspect is neglected. Costs and gains have to be compared by the firm and the candidates with the best ratio are the workforce who secures the production.

Nonetheless, non-pecuniary aspects are also important for firms considering their staff. With good non-pecuniary working conditions, the personnel is more motivated, more balanced and so more productive. Hence, good circumstances by the certain firm for their employees increase motivation, reduce on-the-job search and thus decrease the quitting rate by them, too. Furthermore, considering the importance of non-pecuniary aspects for workers, good circumstances in a firm can help to hire the best new employees. Hence, a close look for non-pecuniary aspects by the firm might help to become a powerful position in the market because the currently employed workers have as well an intention to stay in the firm as the best unemployed workers want to join. In addition, firms could headhunt the best employees of competing firms with for instance a good firm climate. Best examples for this headhunting are the above-mentioned employee referrals that also increase the pool of new possible applicants. But like many other aspects in labor market matching, this one has advantages and disadvantages. False hiring through employee referrals can lower the quality of worker relations and hence result in a lower productivity.

All in all, pecuniary aspects are important for employees and employers as well as non-pecuniary ones. Both have to be balanced to gain as much as possible - as a worker and as a firm.

References

Acemoglu, D. and A. Wolitzky (2011). "The economics of labor coercion." Econometrica **79**(2): 555-600.

Akerlof, G. A., et al. (1988). "Job switching and job satisfaction in the US labor market." Brookings papers on economic activity: 495-594.

Akerlof, G. A. and J. L. Yellen (1986). Efficiency wage models of the labor market, Cambridge University Press.

Allen, J. and R. Van der Velden (2001). "Educational mismatches versus skill mismatches: effects on wages, job satisfaction, and on‐the‐job search." Oxford economic papers **53**(3): 434-452.

Bagozzi, R. P. (1992). "The self-regulation of attitudes, intentions, and behavior." Social psychology quarterly: 178-204.

Bailey, T. and R. Waldinger (1991). "Primary, secondary, and enclave labor markets: A training systems approach." American Sociological Review: 432-445.

Becker, G. S. (1973). "A theory of marriage: Part I." The Journal of Political Economy: 813-846.

Beishon, S., et al. (1995). Nursing in a Multi-ethnic NHS, Policy Studies Institute London.

Benhabib, J. and C. Bull (1983). "Job search: The choice of intensity." The Journal of Political Economy: 747-764.

Bertrand, M. and S. Mullainathan (2003). Are Emily and Greg more employable than Lakisha and Jamal? A field experiment on labor market discrimination, National Bureau of Economic Research.

Black, M. (1980). "Pecuniary implications of on-the-job search and quit activity." The Review of Economics and Statistics: 222-229.

Black, M. (1981). "An empirical test of the theory of on-the-job search." Journal of Human Resources: 129-140.

Blanchard, O. J., et al. (1989). "The beveridge curve." Brookings papers on economic activity: 1-76.

Blau, G. J. (1985). "Relationship of extrinsic, intrinsic, and demographic predictors to various types of withdrawal behaviors." Journal of Applied Psychology **70**(3): 442.

Böckerman, P. and P. Ilmakunnas (2004). "Job disamenities, job satisfaction, and on-the-job search: is there a nexus." Labour Institute for Economic Research, Finland. Discussion Papers **208**.

Bridges, W. P. and W. J. Villemez (1986). "Informal hiring and income in the labor market." American Sociological Review: 574-582.

Burdett, K. and K. L. Judd (1983). "Equilibrium price dispersion." Econometrica: Journal of the Econometric Society: 955-969.

Carrell, M. R. and N. F. Elbert (1974). "Some personal and organizational determinants of job satisfaction of postal clerks." Academy of Management journal **17**(2): 368-373.

Castilla, E. J. (2005). "Social networks and employee performance in a call center." American Journal of Sociology **110**(5): 1243-1283.

Clark, A., et al. (1996). "Is job satisfaction U‐shaped in age?" Journal of occupational and organizational psychology **69**(1): 57-81.

Clark, A. E. (1997). "Job satisfaction and gender: why are women so happy at work?" Labour economics **4**(4): 341-372.

Clark, A. E. (2005). "Your money or your life: Changing job quality in OECD countries." British Journal of Industrial Relations **43**(3): 377-400.

Clark, A. E. and A. J. Oswald (1996). "Satisfaction and comparison income." Journal of public economics **61**(3): 359-381.

Cohn, E. and S. P. Khan (1995). "The wage effects of overschooling revisited." Labour economics **2**(1): 67-76.

Cornelißen, T. (2009). "The interaction of job satisfaction, job search, and job changes. An empirical investigation with German panel data." Journal of Happiness Studies **10**(3): 367-384.

Davis, S. J. and J. Haltiwanger (1991). Gross job creation, gross job destruction and employment reallocation, National Bureau of Economic Research.

Duncan, G. J. and S. D. Hoffman (1982). "The incidence and wage effects of overeducation." Economics of Education Review **1**(1): 75-86.

Faberman, J. and B. Mazumder (2012). Is there a skills mismatch in the labor market? Chicago Fed Letter. **300**.

Fenoaltea, S. (1984). "Slavery and supervision in comparative perspective: A model." The Journal of Economic History **44**(03): 635-668.

Fernandez, R. M., et al. (2000). "Social capital at work: Networks and employment at a phone center." American Journal of Sociology: 1288-1356.

Gal, S., et al. (1981). "A compound strategy for search in the labor market." International Economic Review: 597-608.

Granovetter, M. (1995). Getting a job: A study of contacts and careers, University of Chicago Press.

Granovetter, M. S. (1973). "The strength of weak ties." American Journal of Sociology: 1360-1380.

Hartog, J. (2000). "Over-education and earnings: where are we, where should we go?" Economics of Education Review **19**(2): 131-147.

Hartog, J. and H. Oosterbeek (1988). "Education, allocation and earnings in the Netherlands: Overschooling?" Economics of Education Review **7**(2): 185-194.

Heckman, J. (1974). "Shadow prices, market wages, and labor supply." Econometrica: Journal of the Econometric Society: 679-694.

Hersch, J. (1991). "Education match and job match." The Review of Economics and Statistics: 140-144.

Herzberg, F. and B. P. Mausner (1957). "RO & Capwell, DF (1957)." Job attitudes: Review of research and opinion.

Hodson, R. (1989). "Gender differences in job satisfaction." The Sociological Quarterly **30**(3): 385-399.

Holmstrom, B. and P. Milgrom (1991). "Multitask principal-agent analyses: Incentive contracts, asset ownership, and job design." Journal of Law, Economics, & Organization: 24-52.

Hulin, C. L. and P. C. Smith (1965). "A linear model of job satisfaction." Journal of Applied Psychology **49**(3): 209.

Kagel, J. H. and A. E. Roth (2000). "The dynamics of reorganization in matching markets: A laboratory experiment motivated by a natural experiment." Quarterly Journal of Economics: 201-235.

Kahneman, D., et al. (1999). Well-being: Foundations of hedonic psychology, Russell Sage Foundation.

Kristensen, N. and N. C. Westergård-Nielsen (2004). Does low job satisfaction lead to job mobility?, IZA Discussion paper series.

Laffer, A. B. (2004). The Laffer curve: Past, present, and future, Executive Summary Backgrounder.

Lay, C. H. and R. Brokenshire (1997). "Conscientiousness, procrastination, and person-task characteristics in job searching by unemployed adults." Current Psychology **16**(1): 83-96.

Lee, R. and E. R. Wilbur (1985). "Age, education, job tenure, salary, job characteristics, and job satisfaction: A multivariate analysis." Human Relations **38**(8): 781-791.

Lévy-Garboua, L., et al. (2007). "Job satisfaction and quits." Labour economics **14**(2): 251-268.

Lin, N., et al. (1981). "Social resources and strength of ties: Structural factors in occupational status attainment." American Sociological Review: 393-405.

Liu, W. T. and R. W. Duff (1972). "The strength in weak ties." Public Opinion Quarterly **36**(3): 361-366.

Marsden, P. V. and E. H. Gorman (2001). Social networks, job changes, and recruitment. Sourcebook of labor markets, Springer: 467-502.

Mas-Colell, A., et al. (1995). Microeconomic theory, Oxford university press New York.

Mattila, J. P. (1974). "Job quitting and frictional unemployment." The American Economic Review: 235-239.

McCormick, B. (1990). "A theory of signalling during job search, employment efficiency, and "stigmatised" jobs." The Review of Economic Studies **57**(2): 299-313.

Morgan, P. and R. Manning (1985). "Optimal search." Econometrica: Journal of the Econometric Society: 923-944.

Mortensen, D. T. (1986). "Job search and labor market analysis." Handbook of labor economics **2**: 849-919.

Mortensen, D. T. and C. A. Pissarides (1994). "Job creation and job destruction in the theory of unemployment." The Review of Economic Studies **61**(3): 397-415.

OECD (2005) Skills mismatch.

Oshagbemi, T. (1997). "Job satisfaction and dissatisfaction in higher education." Education+ Training **39**(9): 354-359.

Peacock, L. (2013) Economic downturn has made jobs 'skills mismatch' worse, says ILO.

Phelps, E. S. (1968). "Money-wage dynamics and labor-market equilibrium." The Journal of Political Economy: 678-711.

Pissarides, C. A. (1990). Equilibrium unemployment theory, MIT press.

Quinn, R. P. and G. L. Staines (1979). "The 1977 quality of employment survey: Descriptive statistics, with comparison data from the 1969-70 and the 1972-73 surveys."

Rogers, E. M. and D. K. Bhowmik (1970). "Homophily-heterophily: Relational concepts for communication research." Public Opinion Quarterly **34**(4): 523-538.

Rohrbach-Schmidt, D. and M. Tiemann (2011). "Mismatching and job tasks in Germany–rising over-qualification through polarization?" Empirical research in vocational education and training **3**(1): 39-53.

Roth, A. E. and X. Xing (1994). "Jumping the gun: Imperfections and institutions related to the timing of market transactions." The American Economic Review: 992-1044.

Rousseau, D. M. and J. McLean Parks (1993). "The contracts of individuals and organizations." Research in organizational behavior **15**: 1-1.

Rynes, S. L., et al. (1991). "The importance of recruitment in job choice: A different way of looking." Personnel psychology **44**(3): 487-521.

Saleh, S. D. and J. L. Otis (1964). "Age and level of job satisfaction." Personnel psychology **17**(4): 425-430.

Saloner, G. (1985). "Old boy networks as screening mechanisms." Journal of Labor Economics: 255-267.

Salop, S. C. (1973). "Systematic Job Search and Unemployment." The Review of Economic Studies **40**(2): 191-201.

Sattinger, M. (1995). "Search and the efficient assignment of workers to jobs." International Economic Review: 283-302.

Shields, M. A. and S. W. Price (2002). "Racial harassment, job satisfaction and intentions to quit: evidence from the British nursing profession." Economica **69**(274): 295-326.

Shimer, R. and L. Smith (2000). "Assortative matching and search." Econometrica **68**(2): 343-369.

Sicherman, N. (1991). "" Overeducation" in the Labor Market." Journal of Labor Economics: 101-122.

Simon, C. J. and J. T. Warner (1992). "Matchmaker, matchmaker: The effect of old boy networks on job match quality, earnings, and tenure." Journal of Labor Economics: 306-330.

Smith, L. (2006). "The marriage model with search frictions." Journal of Political Economy **114**(6): 1124-1144.

Sterling, A. D. (2014). "Friendships and search behavior in labor markets." Management Science.

Stigler, G. J. (1961). "The economics of information." The Journal of Political Economy: 213-225.

Van der Velden, R. K. and M. Van Smoorenburg (1997). The measurement of overeducation and undereducation: self-report vs. job-analyst method, Research Centre for Education and the Labour Market, Faculty of Economics and Business Administration, Maastricht University.

Van Ophem, H. (1991). "Wages, nonwage job characteristics and the search behavior of employees." The Review of Economics and Statistics: 145-151.

Varian, H. R. and R. Buchegger (1991). Grundzüge der Mikroökonomik, Oldenbourg.

Viscusi, W. K. (1980). "Sex differences in worker quitting." The Review of Economics and Statistics: 388-398.

Ward, M. E. and P. J. Sloane (2000). "Non - pecuniary Advantages Versus Pecuniary Disadvantages; Job Satisfaction Among Male And Female Academics In Scottish Universities." Scottish Journal of Political Economy **47**(3): 273-303.

Warr (1999). "Weath-being in the Workplace. In Kahneman, Daniel, Edward Diener, and Norbert Schwarz, eds. Well-being: Foundations of hedonic psychology." Russell Sage Foundation: 392 - 412.

Weiss, A. (1980). "Job queues and layoffs in labor markets with flexible wages." The Journal of Political Economy: 526-538.

Yusuf, S. (2009). "From creativity to innovation." Technology in Society **31**(1): 1-8.

References from Internet

www.social.science.exteen.com (2011), The Business Cycle, http://social-science.exteen.com/20110123/the-business-cycle, detection from 16.11.2014

Copyright 2018 – Alle Rechte vorbehalten

Impressum

Christoph Martinetz
Schützenhofstraße 38
07743 Jena
Deutschland
Covergestaltung: Christoph Martinetz, Coverfoto pixabay.com:

christoph.martinetz@web.de

www.ingramcontent.com/pod-product-compliance
Lightning Source LLC
Chambersburg PA
CBHW071558220526
45469CB00003B/1059